The Polished Professional:

The Essential Business Style and Etiquette Handbook

Edited by National Press Publications

NATIONAL PRESS PUBLICATIONS

A Division of Rockhurst University Continuing Education Center, Inc.
6901 West 63rd Street • P.O. Box 2949 • Shawnee Mission, Kansas 66201-1349
1-800-258-7248 • 1-913-432-7757

National Press Publications endorses nonsexist language. In an effort to make this handbook clear, consistent and easy to read, we have used "he" throughout the odd-numbered chapters and "she" throughout the even-numbered chapters. The copy is not intended to be sexist.

***The Polished Professional: The Essential Business Style
and Etiquette Handbook***

Published by National Press Publications, Inc.
Copyright 2000 National Press Publications, Inc.
A Division of Rockhurst University Continuing Education Center, Inc.

Printed in the United States of America

1 2 3 4 5 6 7 8 9 10

ISBN 1-55852-269-7

Table of Contents

INTRODUCTION

The aim of this book is to acquaint you with current business etiquette.

Like any other skill, practice makes for greater proficiency. The more you use politeness and consideration for others, the more those behaviors will become a part of the natural, normal, real you. Showing respect for others will let others know that you respect yourself and that you expect them to respect you in return.

Social skills are especially important for those looking to advance their careers.

Whether you are dealing with peers, clients, subordinates or superiors, knowing what to do and how to do it increases your self-confidence and lets people know that you are a mature, sophisticated individual who will not act awkwardly or embarrass others.

Remember:

The goal of good etiquette is to bring out the best in the people you encounter and make them feel comfortable in your presence.

Rude, crass, crude, vulgar behavior puts people off. It makes them want to avoid contact with you and may set you up for an equally rude, crude response. You may be brilliant at your job, but poor people skills will hamper your ability to let others see and appreciate your worth. Social skills enable people to work together with ease, cooperation and a desire to please, in an atmosphere of minimal friction. Simple courtesies like saying "please" and "thank you," not interrupting when others speak and using appropriate body language will give you a reputation of politeness that will draw people to you.

Many people confuse etiquette with those strict rules of behavior that make us feel nervous, awkward or uncouth. Some people have used etiquette in the past to display their superiority or put others down. In today's society, we have little use for such snobbish, elitist behavior.

We are more sensitive to cultural differences, more willing to accept the ideas and expressions of others, more tolerant of unusual, out-of-the-ordinary situations.

Those who deal with overseas contacts are much more open, nowadays, to learning about the etiquette and expectations of other cultures. It has been rightly said that learning something of the manners of other races is more helpful to forming good business relationships with them than learning their language.

At home or abroad, inappropriate behaviors can ruin business relationships before they get started. You have a very short time to make that excellent first impression you want others to have of you. Your appearance tells people a lot about you before you speak. Your dress, stance, expression, attitude, style, gestures and body language all help create that important first impression that matters so much. But what then? We've all heard that joke when the frustrated spouse or parent says, "I can dress him up, but I can't take him anywhere."

Manners, good etiquette, knowing what to do and what to say enable you to complete the picture your first impression presented. You looked great, you showed self-confidence, you smiled, made eye contact and shook hands firmly while giving your name clearly. The polished professional keeps the ball in the air. Natural good manners, respect for others, and the ability to put others at ease while remaining comfortable oneself will separate those who truly understand the essentials of business etiquette from those who still have more to learn.

Note: Politeness is an "equal opportunity" skill. None of the recommendations suggested in this book are intended to apply or refer more to one gender than the other. Sometimes the words "he/him" will be used, sometimes "she/her." None of the text is intended to reflect sexist attitudes. Such attitudes are completely inappropriate in the modern business world.

What's Your E.Q.?

As with any skill, it helps to evaluate your proficiency level before you begin training. Areas where you know you have knowledge gaps are good places to start building up your ability level. Test your EQ (Etiquette Quotient) to discover the areas you will profit from exploring first.

This quiz is designed to be a self-evaluation tool. You may find some of the questions "tricky," but they are all questions dealing with areas of etiquette that may cause problems in business.

1. You see a vaguely familiar face while networking at a reception. What should you do?

    a. Ignore the person in case he is someone you should remember.

    b. Say hello and pretend to know the person's name, hoping he will give you clues to his identity.

    c. Walk up to the person and ask if he remembers you.

    d. Introduce yourself.

2. A colleague has introduced you to Mr. Brown. His name tag reads John Brown. How do you address him?

   _____

3. How do you greet a visitor who has just entered your office?

   a. Call out a casual greeting and finish your present task.

   b. Lean across the desk and shake hands.

   c. Stand to greet him and indicate a chair.

   d. Let him choose a seat for himself.

4. You are at a company party. The company president and his wife come to your table. You have met them both before. They are both a lot older than you are. Whom do you greet first, and what should you do about shaking hands?

   a. The CEO: _____

   b. The wife: _____

5. You are collecting some files from an associate's office when the telephone rings. Thinking it may possibly be your colleague with further instructions, you pick it up. It is a client. How do you answer the phone?

   a. Tell the caller that Jack is out right now and to call back later.

   b. Let the caller know that he has reached Jack's office, give him your name, and give him the option of leaving a message or calling again later.

   c. Tell him that Jack is recovering from a hernia operation and won't be able to deal with the problem for at least another week.

   d. Let him talk to you without letting him know that you are not Jack.

6. The cell phone in your briefcase rings in the middle of a training seminar. What do you do?

    a. Glare pointedly at the person sitting beside you until the ringing stops.

    b. Run outside as quickly as you can to catch the caller before he hangs up.

    c. Switch off the phone and apologize quietly to those around you.

    d. Apologize to the speaker at the break.

    e. Answer the call in a low voice to cause the least possible disturbance.

7. An associate asks you to dinner at his home. Should you take a gift?

    _____ YES   _____ NO

8. You have received an invitation to a business reception that is marked RSVP. You are tentatively scheduled to leave on a business trip that day. What should you do?

    _____

9. You have invited a group of associates to lunch. Who should lead the group to the table?

    a. The women in the group will go first in order of seniority.

    b. The most important person will go first regardless of gender.

    c. You will go first regardless of gender because you are the host.

10. You are standing with a group of businesspeople all known to you, but not to each other. You have momentarily drawn a blank on one person's last name. What do you do?

    a. Ask that person to remind you of his name so that you can make introductions.

    b. Hope that they will all introduce themselves if you say nothing.

    c. Pretend that you do not know that they are strangers.

    d. Introduce them by their first names only.

11. You are at a business dinner with upper managers and clients. You are one of the first to be served. You are very hungry and hate to let your food get cold. May you begin to eat right away?

    _____ YES   _____ NO

12. You are hosting a business dinner. The important guests have been served and so have you. Only a couple of junior executives are still waiting. Should you go ahead with the signal to begin so that the important guests are not kept waiting?

    _____ YES   _____ NO

Check your score on the next page.

Answers to EQ Quiz

How did you do?

1. d

2. Mr. Brown

3. c

4. Greet the wife first, but do not offer to shake hands unless she initiates the gesture.

5. b

6. c and d

7. YES. It is always appropriate to take a small gift when visiting someone's home.

8. Respond quickly by calling and explaining your dilemma. Ask if you may delay making a firm reply until you are more certain about your schedule.

9. c

10. a

11. NO. It is impolite to start before all are served. If there is a specific reason, such as having to leave early, for you to be given permission by the host to begin before all are served, then you should excuse yourself to the other diners before going ahead.

12. NO. Important guests may be served first as a mark of respect, but all guests should be served before beginning to eat. The host indicates when to begin by unfolding the napkin and by picking up utensils. Hosts are usually served last. If for some reason the host's meal is delayed for several minutes, then the host may give guests permission to begin, but never do hosts give permission to themselves to begin before all their guests are served.

Note: It is not the intention of this quiz to trip you up. Some of the questions are tricky, but they are not trick questions. Each topic reflected in the questions is covered in-depth in this book. It is suggested that you improve your skills by turning to those sections of the book that deal with answers you felt least sure about and read those first. Other sections can be used for reference or confirmation.

Assessing your expertise is helpful to you in discovering where you need to apply more skills training. Improve your Etiquette Quotient by familiarizing yourself with what constitutes good manners in today's business world.

Coaching note: This book may also be used as a training tool for new employees or for those you are coaching. If you are a mentor, this may be a good instrument to start your protégé off on the right foot on his climb up the corporate ladder.

1 MAKING THAT FIRST IMPRESSION

Did you know that you only have seven seconds to make a first impression? That's right — seven seconds! That's all the time it takes for someone to size you up — give you the "once over" — and make a decision about you, your professionalism, your expertise, your self-confidence and your appearance. Making a lasting, good impression is important, but if we fail to get off to a good start in that crucial first seven seconds, we may lose the chance to build a relationship of value later.

Ten Suggestions for Creating the First Impression You Want to Make

1. **A clean, neat appearance** — goes without saying.

   - It's hard to believe how many people still show up for a business appointment with unwashed hair, "five o'clock shadow" (suitable only for television stars!), dirty fingernails, stained ties or blouse fronts, scuffed shoes, hems hanging, buttons missing and other signs of lack of concern for personal hygiene and appearance. People who look dirty or untidy are distasteful to others. Most people don't want to reach out a hand to such a person. They'll start to wonder more about the person's appearance than about what he's saying.

2. **Appropriate clothing** — will help you feel like part of the group.

- Some people send confusing signals by trying to look too youthful, trendy, fashionable or wealthy, by "dressing up" to play the part.

- Most people are not fooled for long by someone acting a part that is not his normal role.

- You do not have to be well-off to dress appropriately for business.

- It is always better to err on the side of conservativeness rather than to be too casual, especially when starting a new job or beginning your career.

- Wear quiet, darker colors and simple, comfortable, well-made clothing in natural fibers for the look that says you want people to see you, rather than the suit you have chosen.

3. **Learn to listen** — good listeners are a rarity.

- The single, greatest psychological need of all human beings is to have someone who will really listen to them.

- Learn good listening skills. Apply body language such as eye contact, leaning forward and nods to let others know you are attentive.

- When meeting someone, don't rush in to talk. People who rush in to speak first on every occasion may appear overeager, egotistical and uncaring.

- Listening enables us to assess the situation, evaluate what needs should be met first, and discover what is really going on.

- We can make better decisions and approach people from a position of knowledge when we spend time listening first. Most of all, if you don't know the person, listen carefully for his name. Getting the name wrong once is understandable; continually getting it wrong is just poor manners.

4. **Smile** — unless it is a very serious occasion, smiling in a warm, friendly manner is a good approach mode.

    •   Avoid huge grins, inane laughter or showing too many teeth. Some cultures regard flashing teeth as signs of aggression; others find it phony. Avoid overdoing it by smiling warmly as you respond to the greetings, shake proffered hands and mentally file away the names of those you are meeting for the first time.

5. **Disconnect** — your cell phone or pager.

    •   If you must be able to be paged, then choose a silent, pulsing type of pager that stores the return number for you to get a message later. If you absolutely must be in contact, then warn those you are just meeting for the first time of the problem and apologize in advance for any disturbance you may cause. "Cell rage" is becoming as much of a social phenomenon as "road rage" and "air rage."

6. **Relax** — tension is catching. If you want others to feel comfortable, stand straight, keep your shoulders loose and feel comfortable yourself. Focusing on the other person is a good way to prevent feeling self-conscious. To give a strong impression of assertiveness, try the "power pose":

    •   Shoulders down and relaxed

    •   Head and chin slightly up

    •   Eyes straight ahead and making eye contact briefly

    •   Hands relaxed at sides — not clenched

    •   Feet firmly planted about 8"-12" apart

7. **Avoid fidgeting** — it suggests you are nervous or not paying attention.

   - Get a friend to critique you, or watch an informal video of yourself if you suspect you may have some bad habits that need correcting.

   - Biting nails or chewing the inside of the cheek are common symptoms of fidgety nervousness.

   - Some people try to avoid twisting buttons or cracking their knuckles by keeping their hands in their pockets, but this is not good etiquette either.

   - If you have trouble keeping your hands still, carry a folder or notebook in your hands.

   - Be careful of playing with your pen — especially clicking a ballpoint on and off.

8. **Wait until your host invites you to sit** — plunking yourself down before it has been indicated that you may proceed is an example of poor manners.

   - If the host tells you to be seated, and it is unclear which seat you should take, thank him for the invitation and ask which seat he would like you to take.

9. **Prepare** — by knowing something about the person you are meeting and his company.

   - Make sure that you have the correct names of those present.

   - Prepare for any cultural differences that could create problems.

   - Introduce yourself clearly and have your business card in a holder in your pocket, so that you can supply one quickly and easily if your host requires one.

- Use the person's name when greeting him and never use first names unless given permission to do so, especially with older, more senior people and clients.

10. **Be punctual** — you don't have to be there to make a bad first impression; you can do it just by being late.

Manners: Social conduct; etiquette; especially polite and civil social behavior.

Funk and Wagnalls, Standard Desk Dictionary

Summary

- It only takes seven seconds to make a first impression.

- Be aware that in those seven seconds, others are looking at your face, your body language and your clothing and listening to your words, your tone and your voice pitch.

Think about someone you've met recently whom you didn't know before. What did he look like?

- Facial appearance

- Clothing

What did he sound like?

- Voice tone

- Voice pitch

What did he say to you in the first few seconds?

What was your initial impression of this person and what do you believe made you form that impression?

Reflections

2 SAYING HELLO AND SAYING GOODBYE

Greetings and Goodbyes

It is common courtesy to greet people you work with in an open, friendly manner as the working day begins. All too often, bad attitudes and poor working relationships are fostered by grumpy behavior, setting an unhappy mood at the start of the day. Instituting a custom whereby everybody greets co-workers with a friendly "hello" helps get the day off to a good start. Similarly, saying "goodbye" when leaving will let others know that you are going and will provide closure to the day.

To Shake or Not to Shake? The All-Important Handshake Question

A handshake is such an important part of the North American ritual of greeting in business, and yet it is fraught with uncertainty and anxiety for many people. When is it appropriate to extend your hand for a handshake? Should you wait until the other person extends her hand first? Do women shake hands with each other? What about an older person? A younger person? Who goes first? How firm a handshake? How long should I maintain contact? The questions go on.

A handshake may well be a part of that all-important good first impression you want to make. A handshake is a communication tool. Your handshake can affect the way others feel about you and about themselves. In our society, we tend to think of the handshake as a sign of goodwill and greeting. In other societies, a handshake is a bond, a token that a deal has been made, a gesture of respect, congratulation or affection. It is important to remember that handshakes create an actual physical bond between individuals, which, although brief, is still a powerful method of conveying complex and far-reaching information.

Handshakes are customary in our society when we meet new people or are reacquainted with someone after an absence of some time. Some European cultures have people shake hands more frequently. In ancient times, handshakes were a signal that the greeters were unarmed, harmless and well-intentioned toward each other. In today's society, we still send signals through our handshakes. A firm, brisk, brief handshake is often considered a sign that the person greeting us is a dynamic, assertive individual. Limp, damp handshakes can send just the opposite signal.

Handshake hitches occur when we fail to be sensitive to those we greet. Some cultures do not customarily shake hands. Take the lead from the host or the most important person present.

Not all older women shake hands as readily as do men of all ages. Wait for the older woman to initiate the handshake before reaching out to take her hand. People with disabilities may have difficulty shaking hands. Once again, it avoids embarrassment if you wait for them to initiate or observe how they greet others before making your move.

Many older people have arthritis, so don't overdo the hearty handshake if you suspect it may be painful for the recipient. It is possible to present that dynamic image with a more gentle grasp if need be.

High-fives and other "cool" handshake styles are fun and have their place in today's business culture. However, meeting new people in regular business situations and especially greeting superiors or new clients require a simple, straightforward, right-handed shake. Save the fun salutations for people you know, team-building times or informal social occasions.

Always stand when shaking hands.
Exception:
**When seated at a formal dinner,
remain in your chair to greet immediate neighbors.
Acknowledge those farther away with a smile.**

Avoid shaking hands across the table or group, if possible. Walk around and stand beside the person to whom you have just been introduced. Try to keep your right hand free at social events where food or drinks are served so that you can shake hands easily with those you meet. This is doubly important if you have been holding sticky, messy food or a wet, cold glass.

If you know you suffer from sweaty palms, use an antiperspirant or dusting of baking soda on your palms and keep a cotton handkerchief in your pocket. Beware of tissues. They can stick to a damp palm and be inadvertently passed over to the person with whom you are shaking hands.

It is better to remove gloves before shaking hands. If your hands are very cold, you may want to issue a warning before going ahead, just as long as you don't blow on them first. This is unsanitary and, like offering a hand you have just used to smother a sneeze, very offensive to others.

Saying Goodbye or How to Leave Gracefully

Goodbye can be harder to accomplish gracefully than making the initial greeting.

If you have asked another person for a meeting with a specific agenda and/or time frame, stick to it. Nothing is more annoying than begging for five minutes and then taking an hour. It is inconsiderate and gives the impression right away of an uncaring, disorganized, insensitive person with poor manners.

Leaving without saying goodbye is socially inept. Others may waste time looking for you, believing that you're still in the area. So even if it is simply a case of sticking your head around a door and saying, "I'm off now, goodbye everyone," rounding off the day or the session with a word of farewell is the polite thing to do.

Try to avoid angry, unpleasant conclusions to the day. If you have disagreed with a person, recap some of the areas where there was agreement, agree to disagree, and arrange to meet later to solve the problem. Making a friendly farewell will let the other person know that you are not taking it personally but are being assertive in keeping the lines of communication open.

Negative attitudes at work are often fostered by people ending the day with unresolved conflict. They stew about it at home and then bring the conflict to work the next day, escalating it into a major crisis. Having customs established in the workplace that encourage people to end their day with friendly farewells that put workday problems aside and focus on strengthening relationships is a good prevention against negative attitude build-up.

Some Goodbye Issues

1. Knowing When to Say Goodbye

Read the body language of the person you are meeting with. If she is indicating through fidgeting, looking at the clock or other signs of boredom that she wants to end the interview, bring things to a close and leave as soon as possible. Outstaying your welcome is a sure way not to be asked back. Ask for another appointment if necessary to conclude unfinished business.

2. Electronic Communication

What if you don't want to have the next meeting in person? In today's business world, personal meetings are not always needed. Electronic communication via the computer or telephone may be preferable. The initial interview will give you information about the individual preferences of the other person. If you are doubtful about the other person's willingness to continue discussions using another medium, ask. Remember to get her permission for changes you want to initiate.

3. The Long Goodbye

However the meeting ends, keep it brief. Stand, smile, thank, shake hands and leave. Long, protracted farewells are unnecessary and tiresome. While you may want to be absolutely sure that you have full understanding, it is not a good idea to recap everything that has been said while standing at the door.

Summary

- Handshakes are part of our North American business culture, but be aware that not every other culture accepts them as readily as we do.

- Wait for the person with the most seniority or the older person to extend her hand first.

- Avoid "cool" handshakes.

- Don't shake so firmly that you cause pain to the other person.

- Remove gloves before shaking hands.

- Always say goodbye when leaving.

- Try not to leave in anger.

- Get permission to conduct an electronic meeting the next time.

- Don't have a protracted goodbye at the door.

Did you know that your voice inflection also creates a strong impression when saying "hello" to another person? Use the following exercise to become aware of this dynamic.

Say aloud, "Hello, how are you?" to the following individuals:

1. Your spouse or partner who has been away for 10 days visiting an ailing parent.

2. The fancy restaurant's head waiter whom you know.

3. Your boss, a "cold fish," whom you run into at the mall.

4. Your doctor.

5. Your secretary, who just arrived late for the meeting.

6. Your party guest, who just arrived a half-hour early.

7. The trash collector.

8. The clerk at the check-out counter in the local convenience store.

9. The newspaper vendor you see every morning.

10. The neighbor's 10-year-old son.

Handshake Awareness:

For the next week, become aware of people who shake hands with you. Use the following questions to form a framework for handshakes:

1. Who proffered their hand first?

2. How firm was the handshake?

3. How long did it last?

4. What kind of body language accompanied the handshake?

Reflections

3 PRECEDENCE — WHO GOES FIRST?

Do you remember the old Chip 'n Dale cartoon in which the two chipmunks argue about who goes first? "After you," says one. "Oh no, after you," says the other. "No, no, you go first," the first replies. "You go first," says the other. In the end, neither chipmunk moves. Do you sometimes feel like that in a business situation? Who goes first? There are distinct rules to deal with these sticky situations.

Many rules of etiquette are based on the order of precedence. In the past, people were extremely concerned with precedence, and even simple house dinner parties involved a careful lineup for going into the dining room with those of most important rank ahead of those of lower social standing.

Precedence is used in business to determine the order in which people are:

- Addressed

- Greeted

- Introduced

- Referred to

- Seated

- Served

Even modern businesses, which tend toward a team structure, still have some sort of hierarchical organization, especially among top management people. Knowing the structure of your own organization is essential. It is also important to know the structure of companies that you deal with on a regular basis, especially clients and partners. Finding out about company structures when you wish to approach a potential client is a wise business practice.

Dealing With Dignitaries

A working knowledge of how to handle social occasions when you, and possibly an escort, may need to mingle with people of rank will help you to cope with potentially difficult encounters with:

- Elected officials

- Appointed officials

- Visiting nobility

- Ecclesiastical leaders

- Higher military ranks

Foreign protocol rules are very complex and should not concern us too much in the normal business scene. If you know that you will be taking part in foreign trade situations and will need to know how to act at diplomatic functions with foreign officials and dignitaries, it is sensible to be well-prepared. Contact the embassy of any country you will visit and ask for their advice.

Here in the United States, it is necessary to know that:

- United States government officials have precedence.

- State officials have higher ranking than do county or city officials.

- Spouses who do not hold office follow immediately behind their officeholder spouses.

(Information on this topic is available from the State Department or governor's office.)

Ladies First?

Although the old rule, "Ladies first," is objected to by many as sexist, it has not totally died out. Women still are generally given precedence over men, as are elders over juniors, both in formal and casual situations. Modern manners suggest that rather than doors being opened by men for women, doors should be opened by the least encumbered for the most encumbered, regardless of gender.

Similarly, it is the host who orders, introduces, indicates precedence of serving and pays when dining out, regardless of gender. The host will introduce and attend to the needs of the individuals, then to the smaller groups before the larger groups at any meeting — social, business or formal — unless dignitaries are present. The needs of dignitaries come before the needs of any other individual or group, large or small.

Although it is still proper to say "ladies and gentlemen" at the start of an address to a group, the word "women/woman" is more accepted now than "ladies/lady."

For example: "Ladies and gentlemen, I would like to thank the woman who instituted this event, Ms. Emily Turner, and recommend her as an inspiring example of what can be accomplished by determined women everywhere." Referring to women as "gals" or "girls" is offensive to most women and totally inappropriate in formal situations.

Similarly, it is better to use "men/man" in general conversation, and "gentlemen/gentleman" when making a speech. Avoid calling men "boys" or "dudes," terms demeaning to all men that may also be considered as racial slurs and not for formal use under any circumstances.

The modern tendency to refer to a group as "you guys" is deplorable. Do not use this term in any but the most casual situations.

Making introductions is a difficult task for most of us. Practice helps, but your most valuable asset is a good memory. Many companies use name tags for their employees, and while this may help you keep tabs on everyone, it is not good manners to stare at a person's lapel while introducing him to others.

Introductions make the business world go around. If you are the senior person present, a host, or simply the only one who knows everybody else in a group, you are obliged to introduce people to each other.

A basic rule is to introduce people of lesser rank to those of more senior rank, or younger to older first. It is a good rule to introduce anyone, regardless of rank, to the client. It is imperative in business to indicate that the customer is the most important person present.

Some older people may prefer to introduce men to women, then women to men, regardless of rank, but this has become less usual in business circles.

If you blank out on a name, you may be tempted to mumble or try to fudge your lapse. It is best to be honest and say something like, "I'm sorry I can't remember your full name, will you please remind me," before attempting the introduction.

If you are the host of a large meeting, you may prefer to invite participants to rise and briefly introduce themselves. This avoids embarrassing mistakes, or the possibility that your memory will let you down. If you choose this option, then it is customary for the host to begin by introducing himself first, and then passing on to the one on his right, and so on around the table.

Failing to introduce makes it difficult for people to converse and is especially awkward if just one person in the group is unaware of the identities of all the rest.

So, think how miserable you would feel in similar circumstances, and go ahead with the introductions. It is better to have inexpert introductions than no introductions at all.

Quite often in such circumstances, it is only necessary to present the newcomer. Others in the group will often then take over the introduction process for you, saying their own names as they shake hands with the new acquaintance. This is an example of the tendency to less formality in business today and also of a willingness of most people to accept that everyone is probably not going to remember their name all the time.

If your host seems ready and able to introduce you, then by all means let him go ahead. If you sense that he is hesitant or reluctant to make the introduction, then you may well conclude that he is feeling embarrassed by a memory loss. Going ahead and introducing yourself is an acceptable alternative in most business situations today.

What to Say When Making an Introduction

You have several choices. The choice you make depends on the situation:

- *Most formal* — "May I present ... ." Use this at the embassy.

- *Formal business* — Say the most distinguished first and last name (add the title if necessary) and then the names of those you wish to introduce to that person after the words: "May I introduce ... ."

- *Casual* — First name of one person, "this is," followed by first name of second person.

Note: The last option is too casual for most business situations.

It is usually helpful to introduce people with reference to their position in the company or relationship to it. An example might be:

"Allen Wainwright, may I introduce our chief of design, Jack Downs. Mr. Wainwright is representing Avis Company for their new site development."

Introducing Groups

Interesting changes happen when we introduce groups. Smaller groups always take precedence over larger groups. If it is a social occasion, and Allen Wainwright's spouse is present, they become the larger group. Even though Allen Wainwright has the chief position of client, the introduction is made to Jack Downs. Allen Wainwright's importance may be highlighted by having her position explained first instead.

"Jack Downs, may I introduce Allen and Janice Wainwright. Mr. Wainwright is the site development representative for Avis Company. Jack is our chief of design."

Always use the person's name, rather than "he" or "she," when describing their role.

Beware of Changing Social Mores

Dealing with introductions of couples can become a social minefield! When introducing a married couple, in the past it was usually only necessary to give one surname.

"May I introduce Janet Newman and her husband, Craig."

Today, many women retain their own last name.

"May I introduce Janet Newman and her husband, Craig Bronski."

Presenting people who are with a significant other who is not a spouse can give rise to confusion. For instance, saying, "May I introduce Janet Newman and her partner, Craig Bronski," does not specify if the pair are in a business or personal relationship.

It is best to avoid terms like "boyfriend" or "girlfriend," which sound coy, but finding some other acceptable phrase may not be easy. Asking the couple how they wish to be introduced is probably the safest solution. If all else fails, leave out the relationship word and simply say, "May I introduce Janet Newman and Craig Bronski." Then, it's up to the introduced couple to clarify their relationship if they wish to do so.

Introductions are tricky, so keep on honing your skills. This is the age of networking, and people are more comfortable introducing themselves than in the past. The fact remains that introductions can and do make the wheels of business turn easier.

A Word of Warning!

Avoid saying "… present *to you* … ." It is very easy to change the precedence order by slipping up and saying, "… present *you to* … " instead.

Say the person's name immediately after "present." As in: "May I present William Brown." It's safer and shorter, a double advantage.

Some General Business Rules

- The level of authority determines precedence.

- When introducing peers of equal rank, give precedence to the longest serving or oldest.

- Clients and customers have precedence, regardless of rank.

- Show proper respect for associates.

A Basic Formula for Introductions

Following the basic formula will be best in most circumstances when formal introductions must be made.

1. Determine the order of precedence.

2. Start with the most important person present, using his full name.

3. Follow this with the introductory statement "May I present" or "May I introduce."

4. Say the other person's/people's name(s) and briefly refer to their role(s). Remember to introduce smaller groups after individuals and before larger groups.

Summary

- Always stand to make introductions or be introduced. That way, you are ready to shake hands.

- If you are unsure of a name or pronunciation of a name, then ask for clarification before you begin.

- Introduce yourself if you are not introduced.

- Keep relaxed, but with your hands out of your pockets. This way, you will be free to shake hands or gesture toward individuals as you introduce them. This may be especially necessary in a large group.

- Avoid going too fast. Give people time to assimilate names. Many people like to repeat the name of someone they just met in order to fix it in their minds.

- Introduce people in the way they want to be known and addressed. If you know your boss prefers to use titles and surnames, then it is better not to continue with first names after the initial mention of the name in the introduction. As you go on with the explanatory part of the introduction, only use titles and surnames. This will let the introduced one know what your boss expects. Do not refer to the boss as "our boss" when explaining his role. Use his title — president, chairperson, the chief executive officer, etc.

- Even if you know the person well and are on a first-name basis, your aim is to introduce him as he wants to be addressed by the person he is meeting.

- Present people at their best, mention new accomplishments such as a promotion or award, but do not refer to personal matters in a business setting. Informing new clients that an associate has just had a baby, bought a new home or been recently married is not appropriate.

- Keep introductions short.

Responding to an Introduction

There's more to do than say "hello" and walk away. Don't let good networking opportunities slip by because of poor follow-through after getting an introduction to someone whom it may be good to get to know.

Important tips for making a good response:

- Stand when being introduced.

- Keep your hands out of your pockets.

- Look at the person to whom you are being introduced.

- Shake hands, unless the person is obviously reluctant to do so.

"How do you do?" is the most formal response. In business it is more appropriate to ask, "How are you?" followed by the person's name. "Hello" and the name are fine for casual introductions. Saying the person's name in the way that he was introduced is polite. Do not go immediately to a first name unless the person breaks into the introduction with an invitation to do so.

Begin the conversation on neutral topics such as the surroundings, unless you are familiar with the person's business, or you have been given plenty of information in the introduction. Do not tell the person you've been "dying to meet him" or are "honored to meet him." This puts you down. Save telling the person it was nice to meet him till you leave.

If you have been introduced incorrectly, then correct the error right away. Some names are hard to pronounce or are easily confused with others. If you are called Ted Green instead of Ed Green by your host, simply say, "My name is Ed Green" while shaking hands. If, however, the introducer fails to let it be known by the introduction that you prefer a more formal address, you need to speak to the introducer after the introductions are over and have him correct the mistake later. This can be awkward. If you are a senior executive who prefers to be addressed as Mr. or Ms., make sure your employees know how to introduce you so that your preference is known. It is not good manners to correct a new employee who was given poor direction. He is not at fault.

> **Make an appropriate comment —
> do not answer the questions
> "How do you do?" or "How are you?"
> during the introduction. Simply repeat them back.**

Tips for Remembering Those Elusive Names

Analogies — Use a resemblance or similarity. For example, a very short person called Little is a good example of using an analogy as a reminder.

Mnemonics — Using a rhyming or similar-sounding word to the person's name that refers to a characteristic of that person is a method many people use to recall names. Because names tend to be abstract, making them more concrete by this sort of linking process is sometimes helpful. For example, a person called Jackson who is frequently out of his office when you call may inspire you to use the mnemonic "action" to remember his name. The problem with mnemonics is that they are often uncomplimentary, and there is a danger of saying the reminder word rather than the person's actual name.

Repetition of the name — is a very good method of fixing it in your mind. Use the person's name as you are introduced and try to use it several times during the conversation. Beware of sounding too much like a political hack when you do this, however, as it is easy to go over the line and appear gushy or phony.

Observation — will help if you are good at names but bad at faces. Registering what the person actually looks like is important. Look at him carefully and try to fix his face in your mind.

Honesty — is vital if you cannot remember a name. Don't try to pretend. Admit your memory lapse and ask for the information you need. People can usually sense if you have forgotten their name and are floundering around for a hint. It is very rare that someone will be offended if you confess your lapse and ask him to tell you again.

Helping those you meet to remember you — is a considerate thing to do, and will encourage the other party to meet you halfway. Say, "Hello, I'm Mark Jones. I believe we met at the Seattle Plumbers Convention." As you extend your hand, the other person will almost always reply with something like, "Yes, I remember. I'm Bill Bland. How are you?" After all, if you forgot Bill's name, it's more than likely he also forgot yours.

Referring to yourself during the conversation is a slightly more subtle way of ensuring that people who you suspect don't recall your name are reminded of it. For example — "You can imagine how pleased I was when my boss announced at the general meeting that I, Jerry Adams, would be going to the Texas office." This is harder to do but is another good method of avoiding embarrassing others who may have forgotten your name. After all, good manners are all about saving others from feeling uncomfortable and awkward.

Check Your Skills

Introduction Opportunity 1.

As marketing director, you want to have potential client Jim Walsh meet with one of your sales staff, Tom Valensky.

Introduction Opportunity 2.

You are purchasing custom online learning programs for your company. The vendor, Archie Jennings, invites you and your boss, Tony Dawson, to lunch.

Introduction Opportunity 3.

Susan Croft has been hired as an accountant. The first step in her orientation is an introduction by you, the chief of finance, to the current accountant, Bob MacIntyre, who will be her peer.

Introduction Opportunity 4.

Jayco representatives, Lynda Reece and Fred Garstairs, have arrived to make a presentation to your company. Office Manager Rita Dechagne, General Manager Lillian Grover and Comptroller Arthur Phipps are ready to listen. You are the introducer.

Reflections

Introduction Expertise

Introduction Opportunity 1.

"Jim Walsh, may I introduce Tom Valenski? As you know, Tom, Jim is one of our favorite clients from L.A. We specifically selected Tom to handle your account, Jim, because he has plenty of experience with construction companies like yours. We wanted you to get our most highly qualified person, because your business is of prime importance to us."

Note: This is a tricky situation. You have chosen to treat a potential client as if he has already come aboard. Underlining the credentials of your subordinate is important, even though it lengthens the introduction somewhat, because you want to let Jim Walsh know you are already thinking of his company as your client and trying to do the very best for him.

Introduction Opportunity 2.

"Tony Dawson, may I introduce Archie Jennings, who has been showing me some of the interesting program ideas his company can produce for our new online training materials.

"Mr. Dawson is our C.E.O."

Note: Tony Dawson takes precedence over the visitor because he is your boss and Archie is a vendor, not a client. Archie should have picked up on your direction to him that Tony Dawson prefers a more formal style of address and will continue to address him as Mr. Dawson as he makes his pitch.

Reflections

Introduction Opportunity 3.

"Bob MacIntyre, may I introduce Susan Croft, who will be working with you in this department."

Note: Bob MacIntyre is shown deference here because of length of service. It is no longer appropriate to defer to the woman, simply because of her gender. You will probably want to elaborate by providing the new colleagues with more information about each other to break the ice, especially if Bob is wary of working with a new associate.

Introduction Opportunity 4.

"I have invited two representatives from Jayco to give us a presentation of their product, which I believe will be helpful to us. Lynda Reece and Fred Garstairs, may I introduce Lillian Grover, our general manager; our office manager, Rita Dechagne; and our comptroller, Arthur Phipps."

Note: Although the Jayco reps are vendors, they get precedence because they are the smaller group. Your people are introduced in order of seniority. It will probably be helpful to gesture toward Lillian and Rita as you say their names, to clarify who is who.

Reflections

4 GOOD COMMUNICATION — THE SPOKEN WORD

Every business professional will agree that the key to success is good communication skills. Knowing how to speak with assertiveness, write with power, listen with empathy and communicate up, down and sideways is essential.

As with the other areas of business, there are rules for communication that will make it easier for you to avoid the pitfalls and traps of poor communication etiquette. From social chitchat to e-mail, knowing how to communicate is your greatest asset.

Social Conversation

While there are many methods of communicating, and each has its preferred etiquette, small talk is still one of the most important and trickiest to do well. There is a fine line between appropriate and inappropriate subject matter, what constitutes too much or too little time spent chatting, and when the conversation needs to switch from general topics to business.

Small talk has its functions:

- To break the ice and put everyone at ease with one another.

- To give those present some common ground from which they can start to form relationships.

- To develop already-formed relationships.

Keeping these functions in mind as you join in the process will help you do it well.

Many people who are very competent and expert when discussing their field of work become diffident and insecure when engaged in social chat. Since a great deal more business seems to be done now in less formal situations, for example, around the breakfast table or while sharing coffee and cookies with the team, some time spent chatting sociably is inevitable. Small talk is used as an icebreaker, especially during meetings between new people who do not know much about one another or, conversely, when old friends meet to catch up.

There is a tendency for people who find the conversation over their heads to clam up and avoid looking foolish by saying nothing. Asking questions, showing an interest, and encouraging the experts to teach you something you did not previously know is the better ploy. It shows that you are a learner, not afraid to admit you don't know everything. It also gives another person the chance to display her proficiency. Most people love to pass on new information. Letting others shine is a major benefit of good manners.

Practice focusing on others so that you are aware of people who are not at ease with small talk. Try to bring them into the conversation. Mentioning awards, achievements and areas of expertise of such individuals can help swing the conversation into an area where they can participate more easily. Similarly, take the opportunity to deflect the conversation away from someone who is hogging the floor. Monologues do not constitute good small talk. If someone, especially a colleague, is boring everyone, try to slip in a deflecting remark that will pass the conversational ball onto a different speaker and a new topic.

Sometimes sports fans make the mistake of slipping straight into a discussion of last night's game. While many people are keen on sports, and most will probably have information of a recent, big event such as the Super Bowl or World Series, it is not safe to assume that everyone present is as enthralled by basketball or hockey as yourself. Watch for indications that any topic you have introduced is not of interest to others and let it drop before their eyes glaze over.

Keep up on the news. *The Wall Street Journal* and several other newspapers have a summary of the most important news events, so you can keep current even if you are very busy. Magazines such as *Time* or *Newsweek* can give you more insight into world events. The news is available 24 hours a day, constantly updated, on the Internet. TV programs such as *"Discovery"* or *"NOVA"* will also help you find material of general interest, if you fear running out of things to talk about.

People like to be complimented for their achievements. If you are aware that someone has been given an award or promotion or has completed a major project, congratulate her sincerely.

Personal compliments are harder to handle. Remarks about appearance are usually inappropriate. Women can and do sometimes compliment each other on dress, hairstyles, color choices, accessories, etc., especially if they know one another fairly well. For example: "Eileen, I just had to come over and tell you how beautiful I think that pin you are wearing looks on that dress."

Similar comments from a man may not be appreciated, unless there are some special circumstances, such as if the man is a jeweler or antique dealer who says, "Ms. Bright, I am intrigued by the exquisite pin you are wearing. Is it an heirloom?" The focus now is on the pin, and an opportunity for an interesting small-talk topic has been presented.

Personal compliments across gender lines can be construed as harassing and are better avoided, unless you know the individual very well. Personal comments about one person to a third party are usually dangerous also.

Flattery and gushy, insincere remarks do not constitute small talk. Most people dislike toadying behavior. People who always agree with the opinion of the most important person present or who put down people of lower rank than themselves are not popular. Others will usually respect you for sticking to your own opinion, as long as you do not browbeat those who disagree with you or try to make converts out of them.

Socializing is not to be seen as an opportunity to get on your favorite hobbyhorse or dazzle others with your knowledge.

> **Reminder —**
> **"He has occasional flashes of silence,**
> **that make his conversation perfectly delightful."**
>
> *Sidney Smith*

Getting others to talk is the sign of a good host. Keeping to "safe" topics will avoid creating negative situations that might harm business relationships.

Subjects to avoid:

- Malicious gossip

- Personal health problems

- Controversial social questions

- Political campaigns

- Religion

- Sex

- Profanity

- Inappropriate jokes and stereotypical comments

- Personal problems

Malicious gossip is different from newsy gossip. News of a personal nature may be exchanged among people who know one another well. Teams often like to exchange newsy gossip at social times together. It may build relationships and forge closer links between individuals. Passing on unpleasant information, items of doubtful veracity, unpleasant or degrading things about others, particularly behind their backs, is always totally inappropriate.

Personal health problems should not be recounted in great detail in business situations. If you have an obvious injury, such as a cast on your leg, then mentioning that you had a fall while skiing and hope to be free of the cast in a few weeks is fine. Discussion of internal problems, a disease that is not apparent or a recent operation is unnecessary.

If you are dining with business acquaintances who urge you to eat something that you know you can't handle, it is all right to say something like, "I know it looks delicious, but I am a diabetic" or "I'd love to have some, but I have a shellfish allergy." Don't go into details of possible, or previous, outcomes of eating the proffered delicacy.

There are a few people who love discussing the latest test, diets, homeopathic remedies and medications. For business purposes, presume that these people are not present and avoid these topics.

Controversial social questions such as abortion, capital punishment and same-sex marriage are interesting and worthy of serious debate, but too important and emotional for small-talk situations where business relationships are being formed. Stick to less highly charged topics that will avoid hurting or giving offense to anyone present.

Political campaigns are dangerous grounds because they remind people of their potential differences. This is contrary to the aim of the business get-together, which is to foster amicable relations. Political topics that reflect patriotic or nationally supportive views are fine. It is all right to wear a button announcing that you voted, just don't get into whom you voted for.

Religion is another highly charged area with plenty of opportunity for people to disagree. All very private topics, like religious views, are best avoided at business meetings.

Sex seems to have become a national obsession lately, but it is far safer to keep the topic out of business meetings if possible. However, sexual harassment is a major concern for many companies today. Inquiries from one company into how others are handling this hot issue are bound to arise. Explaining your company policy might best be shelved to a specified time, where HR people and upper management can get together in a more formal session. This will avoid opening the topic up to general discussion and argument.

Profanity and scatological language are common nowadays, but still inappropriate. It has, in the past, been tempting to junior staff or women coming into a male-dominated work situation to adopt the use of bad language to make them seem like a part of the group. This is not a good idea. Bad language use becomes habitual very quickly and is hard to lose. Acting shocked or demanding that others stop using profanity is not an effective way of dealing with the problem, unless the language use is deliberately aimed to be harassing. Ignoring the bad habit in others, and refusing to become a part of it, is the most effective way of coping.

Inappropriate jokes and stereotypical comments are getting less common in most business settings. People are aware now of a need to be more socially sophisticated. Political correctness can be overdone, but it does help underline and remind us of how inappropriate some things are in a mixed social or business setting. Stereotypical remarks that label, degrade, offend and ignore the well-being of others are increasingly unacceptable. Empathy is our best guide to avoid hurting others by thoughtless social gaffes. Putting yourself in the place of the one put down will help you avoid making politically incorrect remarks, not only at social and business functions but anywhere.

Personal problems, such as your child's poor report card, a failing marriage, or group therapy, which require serious, heavy-duty, intimate information to be disclosed, are definitely not the stuff from which small talk is made. Amusing anecdotes about decorating your home, or short reminiscences about the behavior of a pet, are usually fine, especially if they add to a topic introduced by someone else who will be happy that you have stepped in to keep the conversational ball rolling.

Personal problems that affect your work should only be discussed with your immediate supervisor or HR person, in a private setting.

Speaking Well Helps Your Listeners

Develop an interesting and varied vocabulary. Remember, simple words are more effective than polysyllabic, pretentious ones, particularly if you don't really know their exact meaning or usage.

- Avoid jargon or very technical terms in general conversation.

- Pedantic insistence on very formal or outdated word usage is irritating.

- Overuse of slang words may be offensive to some people.

Our language is constantly evolving, modifying and growing. New words are being invented, words from other cultures are being added, and the meanings of familiar words change over time. Keeping up-to-date can be quite a challenge. Reading and good conversation are still the best ways to polish your verbal skills.

Affectations in speech, such as overtly foreign pronunciation of words from other languages that are commonly used in this country, should be avoided. Words like pizza, champagne or Wiener schnitzel, for example, are in everyday use here and do not need to sound particularly Italian, French or German.

As with many other things in life, simplicity, honesty and a willingness to learn are better guides than affectation, a know-it-all attitude and pretending you are something you are not.

Today's Changing Workplace

There is a blossoming diversity in the workplace today. Global markets are changing almost daily, creating diverse markets and workplaces composed of people from various cultures and backgrounds. Traditionally, business handled diversity by adopting a melting pot myth, but in reality, many of these groups haven't blended in. Today, it is more important than ever to communicate with all types of people in the workplace — young and old, men and women, all races, colors and creeds — and to communicate in a diplomatic and tactful way.

Refer to people from other countries by the name of their country. For example: "Ms. Ng is from Vietnam," rather than "Asia." "Mr. Valdez is visiting us from Bolivia," rather than "South America."

Collective terms used to describe ethnic groups are tricky. African-American or Native American are currently correct ways to refer to people of certain specific ethnic groups. However, these terms change, regionally as well as temporally. If you are unsure of which term is preferred by an individual, then ask politely, explaining that you want to be sure to avoid giving offense.

If you are a member of a particular minority group and you feel you have been incorrectly introduced, you may choose to correct the terminology yourself by saying something like, "Ms. Blake introduced me as a member of the 'Oriental' community here in Grangeton. I would like to make a small correction, if I may, Ms. Blake? My community prefers to be known as the 'Asian-American community' now, as we feel it is more acceptable to the majority of our members." Otherwise, ask Ms. Blake privately to reintroduce you with the preferred description.

Regional accents or phraseology are much more widely accepted today. In the past, people felt that they had to have elocution lessons in order to be accepted by big-city or international companies. Poor grammar is not acceptable, though, so it is still important to avoid pitfalls such as those double negatives, and any tendency to refer to others as "youse."

In the past, people who used accents were labeled by others. Fortunately, stereotyping of this kind is dying out. Nowadays people prefer to hear the variety of regional speech and appreciate differences rather than expect everyone to conform to some bland norm when speaking.

> **"A good listener will get information that a talker will never get. The inside scoop, creative resources, personal information, professional strategies, useful data, and powerful insights into a person's composition come from listening and asking good questions, not in delivering information."**
>
> *Susan Bixler and Lisa Scherrer, "Take Action"*

Summary

- Good communication skills are vital to forming good business relationships.

- Avoid using confusing jargon and technobabble.

- Focusing on others will help reduce self-consciousness.

- Keep up-to-date on current events.

- Use good grammar, but keep those colorful colloquialisms and regional accents that bring life to speech patterns.

- Work on enlarging your vocabulary, but make sure you know exactly what those new words mean and when they should be used.

- Use effective speaking methods that encourage others to listen.

- Practice active listening.

Getting the Knowledge Balance

1. Circle the names of real, not fictional, people:

Jack Armstrong	Steven Jobs	J. Paul Getty
Slim Pickens	J.R. Ewing	Harry Houdini
El Greco	Ed Norton	The Elephant Man
Annie Oakley	Lizzie Borden	Lady Macbeth
Sergeant York	Ichabod Crane	Corporal Max Klinger

2. How about geography? Circle the names of real places:

Timbuktu	Xanadu	Camelot
Bali	Boys Town	Peyton Place
Atlantis	Yemen	Transylvania
Katmandu	Sri Lanka	El Dorado

3. Circle the words that apply to computer technology:

e-mail	motherboard	ram
processor	CPU	bytes
bits	parity	CD-ROM
escape	function key	DVD
baud rate	domain	hypertext
scan	Java	wallpaper
desktop	drive	chip

4. Circle the names of political figures:

Al Gore	John Major	Fidel Castro
Nelson Mandela	Augusto Pinochet	Margaret Thatcher
Jean Chrétien	Corazon Aquino	Benazir Bhutto

Reflections

Reflections

Answers

Question 1:

Jack Armstrong — fictional radio character

Steven Jobs — real — developed "Apple" computer

J. Paul Getty — real — multimillionaire

Slim Pickens — real — television cowboy

J.R. Ewing — fictional TV character

Harry Houdini — real — escape artist

El Greco — real — Spanish painter

Ed Norton — fictional TV character

The Elephant Man — real — John Merrick

Annie Oakley — real — rodeo performer

Lizzie Borden — real — murdered her parents

Lady Macbeth — fictional — Shakespearian character

Sergeant York — real — WWI hero

Ichabod Crane — fictional character

Corporal Max Klinger — fictional TV character

Question 2:

Timbuktu — real

Bali — real

Atlantis — lengendary

Katmandu — real

Xanadu — fictional

Boys Town — real

Yemen — real

Sri Lanka — real

Camelot — legendary

Peyton Place — fictional

Transylvania — real

El Dorado — legendary

Question 3:

They all are related to computer technology.

Question 4:

They are all political figures.

Reflections

5 GOOD COMMUNICATION — THE WRITTEN WORD

More and more people are turning to computer technology to handle all of their written correspondence. Certainly in North America, the majority of corporations are now "wired" with Internet sites and e-mail capabilities. Most companies use fax machines regularly for correspondence. This means that a whole new etiquette is arising for use with these electronic media.

Eight Tips for Good E-Mail Usage

1. Be brief, but remember, the rules of grammar still apply.

2. You have a spell checker. Use it.

3. Use clear addresses and the name of the individual to whom you are sending.

4. Include all other addressees so that the recipient can see where else the message has gone.

5. Some people prefer the use of the third person, rather than personal pronouns, when sending e-mail memos.

6. Use of capitalization indicates that you are shouting when you e-mail a chat room, and some recipients maintain the rule that uppercase should be restricted to really emotional messages only.

7. Beware of sending private messages on networked systems or a computer that automatically sends to everyone on the company, department or team list. There are times when e-mail is not appropriate. A phone call, letter or face-to-face meeting is the better method sometimes.

8. Remember when sending that you seldom have time for a sober second thought. Try to avoid sending when you are very upset.

Note: "Spamming" or sending unsolicited advertising through the Net is very bad manners. Avoid it at all costs.

Faxes

Always use a company fax cover sheet with the appropriate logo, address, phone and fax return numbers, etc. Fill in necessary information such as time, date, sender's name and title so that the recipient knows when you sent the fax, how to get back to you if needed, and the number of pages being sent. It is still a far-from-foolproof system, and the person getting the fax may not realize that he has not received a complete message unless he knows what to expect.

Sending out unsolicited material will annoy recipients who have to pay for incoming faxes.

Faxes of important materials should be followed up by hard copy later. For example, sending your résumé by fax is fine, especially if there is a deadline for receipt; however, send a real copy by mail at the earliest date afterwards. It's the polite thing to do.

Also, faxes can distort copy. Therefore, it makes sense to send hard copies of color brochures or important sales sample materials so the receiver can get the real picture after you have piqued interest with the fax.

Note: There are still plenty of businesspeople out there who dislike electronic communications. They feel uneasy using them and may resent those who use them automatically. It is worthwhile finding out how best to approach clients, customers and valued associates, and using their method of preference. Good manners are all about making the other person feel comfortable.

"Snail Mail"

We once thought that with computers around, written communication would die out, but so far it is still alive and going strong. People still react very positively to the written note that arrives in the mail. In fact, the most important communication is still done by the formal, written, paper delivery method.

Handwritten Notes

Correspondence has been carried out over the millennia using many different materials. Paper and ink are still viable tools for communicating. Today we are very much geared to using electronic communicating methods in the business world. That may well explain the tremendous impact that handwritten notes have on the reader. Nothing says that you took time and trouble to make a personal connection than a letter, card or note that you wrote and sent yourself.

Handwritten notes are perfect for sending thank-you notes, RSVP replies, congratulations and condolences. Many advisors will tell you that there is no other proper alternative to a handwritten communication in these circumstances. Some companies provide business note cards for their employees to use. These should only be used for business connections.

Using a fountain pen or really good ballpoint, with black, blue or brown ink is preferred.

Having a secretary prepare the correspondence and adding a handwritten note with the signature is also a good way of letting the recipient know that you want to make a personal connection. This may be a way to personalize a communication that is being sent to others as well as the main recipient. If this is the case, add the written note after the CC listings to indicate that the message is for this recipient alone.

Invitations

Replies to invitations marked RSVP (the initial letters of the French phrase "répondez s'il vous plaît"), or "please reply," should be made as soon as possible, preferably within a week. Always use the third person when responding to formal invitations. For example:

"Mr. John Good regrets that he is unable to attend the opening at the Ravel Gallery on June 4."

If the invitation has been made by a close acquaintance, a written negative response should be followed by a phone call with a more personal apology for nonattendance and the reasons why you will not be there. A call saying you were pleased with the invitation and are looking forward to the event is also a nice touch when you know the host well.

If you are unsure about being able to attend, but do not want to close the door on a chance to take in the event, do not just wait and respond later. Call or write, explaining that you would very much like to attend but are unable to give a definite answer now, and find out if it is all right to delay the decision or simply come if you are able. It is a good idea to explain why, so that the host does not think you are just hanging on waiting for a better invitation to come along. Acceptable excuses could be an unconfirmed business trip, expected birth of a child or possible date of elective surgery.

Quite often, the RSVP has been asked for simply to give the host a ballpark figure for attendance, and your sitting on the fence will not really matter. What does matter is that you have responded and have given the host the courtesy of acknowledging and appreciating the invitation.

If the invitation demands a definite "yes" or "no," then your host should tell you that this is the case and give you a deadline date for a final response.

Invitations usually let you know by their wording what kind of event you will be attending. Formal invitations are always written in the third person. Slightly less formal invitations will request the honor of your company or cordially invite you to attend.

If "You and Your Guest" are invited, then you may bring one other person with you. If the invitation is for "You and Your Guests," then you may bring as many others along as you wish. Many business invitations between companies are of this nature.

If the invitation is addressed only to you at your home or place of business and invites you alone, then that is the way you should respond.

The invitation will also indicate the type of event. A reception usually includes some refreshments, drinks and/or finger food. Meal invitations are specified. Other functions may include openings of new sites, launching new products, introducing new staff or celebrating important anniversaries. Sending congratulations for such a specific event along with your response is polite.

It is customary when sending out invitations to specify the day and date of the event first and then the time. Some events may include a finish as well as start time. The place where the event is held usually begins with the name of the location followed by an address on the next line.

Requests to respond — "RSVP" or "Respond if you please" — are located at the bottom left of the invitation card and include a name, telephone number and/or address for replies. If there is no specific return information, then reply to the one who sent the invitation at the company address.

Additional information may be added at the end of the invitation on the right side. This will include items such as style of dress, parking arrangements, or if you will need to present the invitation to gain admittance.

Programs, schedules, directions, etc. should be included on a separate sheet.

Starting and Ending Your Note or Letter

Personal notes like formal letters should always begin "Dear ... ." This is not a term of endearment, just the word our society customarily uses for a salutation. Omitting the word "Dear" and beginning with the person's name alone is not acceptable in a letter. If you know the person to whom you are writing well, then use his first name; otherwise, it is better to be more formal than more casual.

Business notes usually end with the words:

- Sincerely

- Sincerely yours

- Respectfully

- Respectfully yours

before the signature.

Casual notes end with the words:

- Warmly

- Cordially

- Fondly

- Yours truly

- Truly yours

before the signature.

Thank-you notes for entertainment shared by you and an escort should include the names of both of you, although it is only written by one person. It is usual to address the note to the person(s) giving the party and to use their first names after the salutation. Exceptions would be if the occasion was very formal or the host(s) were very distinguished or elderly or people who have indicated that they prefer to maintain the use of titles. When writing on behalf of yourself and others, only the writer should sign.

Letters sent through the mail should be sealed. Cards included with gifts or hand-delivered messages should have the flap tucked inside. It is customary to leave notes unsealed even when they are hand-delivered by someone other than yourself. This indicates that you trust the deliverer not to read your letters.

Business Correspondence

Traditional business letters are still very much in evidence despite the plethora of electronic communication media available to us all today. The way business letters are composed and presented may change a little over time, but the basic structure remains much the same from year to year.

The most important thing to remember when composing a business letter is the need for brevity and clarity combined. All business letters should be neat, error-free and professional-looking.

Appearance Is Important

The style of stationery, logo and headings are almost as important in establishing credibility as the content of the letter. There is a present tendency to be more conservative and understated when choosing company stationery than was the case a few years ago. Trends change. The sort of industry, profession, clientele, location, length of establishment, style and preferences of those in authority are all factors in determining the kind of "look" a particular company will choose for its stationery.

If you are able to choose your own stationery, then be sure that you select something that conveys the right message about you and your organization. Select a style that will stand the test of time. Constantly changing your mind about your stationery, logo or letterhead is expensive and suggests you are unstable or unable to make up your mind.

Use company letterhead paper and matching envelopes for all of your business correspondence. Never use business stationery for personal correspondence. It is really inappropriate to apply for a job using the stationery of your present place of employment.

Single-spaced typing on a good word processor is really the only way to produce a modern business letter. Envelopes may be addressed with labels if preferred. Errors must not be hand corrected or deleted. Reprint after correcting the original.

It is amazing how many people do not use the grammar or spell-check functions of their word processors, which make corrections to letters before printing so easy. Handmade corrections and deletions are very unprofessional and should be avoided at all times.

Keep all correspondence on file so that you can quickly retrieve and refer to letters should it be necessary.

Format

Some companies have uniform business-letter formats that they ask all of their employees to use. Sometimes the choice is left to the individual preference of the writer.

Knowing how you want your letters to look so that you can properly instruct your secretary will enable you to present the image you want to show to others. Finding a business-letter style that suits you may be an option.

Business Letter Format 1

Logo/Heading

Company Name (company name and address can be centered)
Company Address

Date

Recipient's Name, Titles (Professional or Courtesy), Company Affiliation
Recipient's Address

Salutation:

Main Text   — Introduction
              — Body
              — Conclusion

Complimentary Closing,

Signature

Typed Name
Title

Attachments:
Enclosures:
CC:

In past times, the style of business letters was very rigidly prescribed. Nowadays it is possible to choose a style and still be "correct."

Business Letter Format 2 (modified flush left)

Logo/Heading

Company Name (company name and address can be centered)
Company Address

Date

Recipient's Name, Titles (Professional or Courtesy), Company Affiliation
Recipient's Address

Salutation:

Main Text — Introduction
— Body
— Conclusion

Closing,

Signature

Name
Title

Attachments:
Enclosures:
CC:

If you are in doubt, several good reference books are available. Strunk and White's *The Elements of Style* is still one of the best references on the market.

All elements of business letters are single-spaced; this includes the addresses.

To decide how much space to put between each element, such as between the date and the recipient's name and address, let good layout and balance be your guide. Normally, two or three blank lines are left between each element; however, on shorter letters you may wish to drop the top margin down and put a little more spacing between the elements to achieve a good visual balance. Try to keep a one-inch margin at the bottom and on the right and left sides.

As with a memo, there are two ways to format the text of a letter: block format and modified block format. Block format begins every paragraph flush with the left margin and leaves an empty line of space between each paragraph. Modified block format indents each paragraph and does not leave an empty line of space between each paragraph. Do not mix block and modified block formats.

Personal Letters

Personal letters are formatted like business letters except that the company logo and name are omitted, of course. Also, omit printing your name and place your address flush left.

A personal letter can be formatted flush left or modified flush left — just like a business letter. The text can be either block format or modified block format.

As with memos and all types of business correspondence, you should take special care to use correct punctuation, an appropriate tone and good grammar. Always identify your audience and plan before you begin to write. Nothing communicates a poorer image of you than bad letter writing.

If you are at all unsure of the proper form of address for the recipient, such as gender, position or title, call a company and ask for information. A business card may help you to get the correct information. People who have unisex names or who only use initials are particularly hard to greet unless they have a professional title such as Dr., which is nongender-specific.

If you have absolutely no idea to whom you are writing, then begin as you might for a memo with "To whom it may concern," instead of the traditional "Dear."

Only use the first name if the person to whom you are sending a business letter is well-known to you. If you are sending on copies of the letter to others, it is more polite to use titles, even though you know the first recipient well.

It is customary to handwrite your own signature using both first and last names. Do not use a courtesy or professional title when signing your name. Academic letters are acceptable following a signature. Courtesy and professional titles should be included in the typed name under the signature so that the recipient will know how to make an appropriate response.

Return addresses on letterheads may include as much information regarding means of response as you wish. Fax and phone numbers, box numbers, locations, branch locations, etc. are all acceptable. The envelope should have the company name and mailing address only on the top left-hand corner. Business envelopes are always 10 inches long and should match the stationery in color and weight.

If you do not have a specific person to send your letter to, then place the company name on the first line and add "Attention: _____ Department" before the address.

Forms of Address

People from the United States are generally known for their open, friendly, casual manner. The average visitor finds people welcoming, helpful and approachable. Usually this easygoing attitude stands us in good stead and is considered an asset when doing business. There is the potential, however, for an overly casual attitude to get us into trouble.

The main problem lies in our language. We have no "formal second person," as do most other major languages. This, along with a tendency to slip instantly into use of first names immediately after introductions have been made, can lead some foreign visitors to find us overly familiar.

Fortunately for us, the English language is already the predominant business-communication language of the world and is increasingly so every day. The movement for business etiquette is toward the North American style, rather than some other style.

This does not mean we have permission to ride roughshod over the sensibilities of others. Consideration for the feelings of others is the key to good manners. Many people still appreciate more formality at the start of a business relationship and find it conducive to establishing and maintaining a stable, professional and cordial atmosphere.

When visiting another country, it is always good to err on the side of formality in manners and stick to formal modes of address until given permission to move to the familiar mode. Some cultures have definitive rituals such as the "Bruderschaft," where both parties drink with crossed arms, to initiate a move to informality. Others may use informal address away from the workplace but revert to formality during business hours. Good research is invaluable if you are to avoid unwittingly giving offense abroad.

Most Common Forms of Address

- *Honorable* — U.S. officials from presidential appointees to federal and state elective officials, judges and mayors.

- *His/Her Excellency* — foreign, high-ranking officials, ambassadors, heads of state.

- *Doctor* (medical) — followed by the last name. In writing, use the first and last name, then initials of the degree.

- *Academic degrees and titles* — address verbally using the most important title. In writing, the academic title is last. Example: Dr Thomas Blank, Chancellor. When speaking, the academic title is first. Example: Chancellor Blank.

- *Ecclesiastical, Reverend* — covers all clergy. The position title is also correct, e.g., Bishop, Metropolitan, Rabbi, Imam, etc., followed by the last name. Degrees should be added after the title and full name when writing. (Note: Always list degrees in the order in which they were received.)

- *Ms.* — is now preferred for all women in business. Many women prefer it at all times and will usually tell you so if you slip up. Mrs. is still acceptable, when writing informally to a couple with the same surname. Miss is reserved for girls and very young women under 16 years of age.

- *Mr.* — is the courtesy title for all men and boys.

- *Esquire* — has been a courtesy title for attorneys, but is now out of use in the U.S. It is still in use for all men in the U.K.

- *Ma'am/Sir* — suitable only when speaking to an acknowledged superior.

Three Rules for Effective Business Writing

1. Be concise.

2. Be direct.

3. Be simple.

The fewer words used the better. North Americans are notoriously pressed for time. Think of a television commercial and work on ways to get your message across in 20 seconds or less. Clear, concise words that convey images or mind pictures are better than long explanations. A letter or memo of more than one page will not be read. Using point form or bulleted lists can help keep it short.

"Say what you mean, ask for what you want."

- Be specific.

- Do not generalize or assume.

- Use names of things and people.

- Be assertive when you write and take responsibility for what you are asking the other party to do.

- "Doublespeak" or putting a "spin" on what is being conveyed is an effort to flimflam the other person. Insincerity will always rebound on you sooner or later. A good business reputation is built on honesty and telling it like it is.

- Choose short, nontechnical, familiar words, unless you are absolutely sure the recipient of your writing will understand jargon or polysyllabic words.

- Short sentences and everyday words are best. Write for the audience that you know you have. If you are unsure of your audience's knowledge level, keep it simple until you find out.

Summary

- Handwritten notes say much more than the written message. They let others know that you have taken the time and trouble to communicate personally.

- It is polite to respond promptly to invitations.

- Overfamiliarity at the start of a business relationship is hard to correct. Better begin on a formal note and move toward informality as the relationship develops.

- Excellent business letters tell the recipient more about your company than the message alone conveys.

- If you are unsure about the correct way to address someone, call the company office and ask. The State Department, library and reference books will all give you needed information about formal modes of address. The Internet is a wonderful resource for this type of information. It will also help you to find out about the prevailing manners in foreign countries you may be visiting.

- It is vital to be sensitive to foreign customs when doing business abroad.

How up-to-date are your writing skills? Here are some editing challenges that will help you assess how clearly you communicate.

Modernize the following expressions:

1. Please advise as to the method of shipment of …

2. In re of your telephone conversation of yesterday, we …

3. Hoping to see you soon, I am …

4. Kindly let us know by May 10th.

5. Please respond at your earliest convenience.

6. In the event that you have an accident …

7. Enclosed please find our order for …

8. At the present writing, we are not …

9. In the event that we will …

10. In accordance with our …

Reflections

Reflections

Answers

1. How do you want us to ship …

2. Concerning your telephone conversation yesterday …

3. I hope to see you soon. Sincerely …

4. Please let us know by …

5. Please respond as soon as possible …

6. If you have an accident …

7. Here is our order …

8. Right now, we are not …

9. If we will …

10. According to our …

Reflections

6 GOOD COMMUNICATION — TELECOMMUNICATION TECHNIQUES

We've come a long way from the time of the "one ringy-dingy" multi-party telephone and operator-patched switchboard. In today's business world, the telephone is still one of the most powerful forms of communication, and as we deal with companies across the country, it is a powerful means for instant results. Every phone call you receive could mean business for your company, success for you and an opportunity to network.

Think back for a moment, to a time when you found a business phone call handled so unprofessionally that you decided to take your business elsewhere. How much money do you think poor telephone techniques have cost companies in a year? It is ironic that the person who answers the phone is often one of the lowliest, lowest-paid employees in the company. This person may not even rate good training to perform what the misguided employer sees as a low-skill task. It is only in relatively recent times that attention has been paid to improving customer-service skills for employees in general. The company that is aware of the importance of making a good impression on callers is usually one that has learned the value of presenting the best image to its customers on the telephone.

Excellent telephone skills are much sought-after. They depend on being able to project all the desired qualities that tell the caller what a terrific person you think they are, what a great individual you are and what a wonderful company they are calling, using only words.

When we communicate face to face, we rely on many factors to understand what the other party is conveying. The majority of our information comes from the person's facial expressions, gestures and tone of voice. Less than 10 percent is conveyed by the words themselves. On the telephone, we are down to tone and words only. No wonder it's hard to excel. Nor do we have much time to make a good first impression. Our tone and the quality of our greeting are enough to establish a good relationship or destroy it.

We may even fail to establish that good relationship by not answering quickly enough, putting people on hold, electronic answering and voice mail.

Other factors such as background noise, bad lines, interruptions, language problems, etc. can also prevent us from making the best of a call.

More sophisticated telephone equipment allows us to screen calls, take and leave messages, identify callers, handle several calls at once, etc. Unfortunately, many people are not comfortable with electronic communications that involve pressing buttons, leaving messages between tones, or being asked to wait because a call is coming in on another line of the person who just called them.

Cell Phones

Cell phones are also very unpopular, especially with those who believe that their use infringes on the comfort of others. Surveys that have been taken suggest that cell phone use does cause inattentive driving.

- 59 percent of people surveyed said they would rather go to the dentist than sit next to a cell phone user.

- 86 percent reported "abhorrence of cell phone use" at the dinner table.

- 88 percent had been disturbed during a meeting.

- 96 percent thought cell phone use very inconsiderate during a movie.

- 98 percent considered use of cell phones inexcusably rude at a funeral.

But, the media have reported instances of theater performances, concerts and religious services being interrupted by cell phones.

It's hard to imagine anyone thinking that the use of a cell phone at any of these events would be considered acceptable behavior. However, the fact remains that many people fail to use even a regular telephone with courtesy. There is a lot of truth to the comment by social observers that manners in general have deteriorated since telephone usage became widespread. Perhaps the imperative ringing of the phone bell is such an effective attention-getter that we have trouble handling it in a sensible fashion.

If you should accidentally leave your cell phone on, and it interrupts a public event, you need to turn it off and apologize at once to those you have disturbed. If a meeting is going on, apologize to the speaker and/or chairperson at the soonest opportunity.

Answering Calls — Yours, Ours and Theirs

Whether you are answering the phone in your own office or taking calls for another, certain rules need to be followed.

Ten Basic Rules When Answering Business Calls Yourself

1. Pick up the handset before the third ring whenever possible.

2. Start with a short, appropriate greeting such as "Good Morning."

3. Identify yourself using your full name and a title if you wish to be addressed that way.

4. Identify your organization.

5. A few general pleasantries are nice but avoid wasting time on extended small talk.

6. Keep an open, neutral tone.

7. Have background noise at a minimum.

8. Always ask permission if you have to put someone on hold.

9. Give options for the caller to either call you back or for you to call her, if you know that a prior caller will be with you for some time.

10. Avoid doing other tasks while taking a call, especially talking to or laughing with someone else in the room.

Five Basic Rules for Answering an Associate's Telephone

1. Only pick up an associate's telephone if you are asked or are expected to do so.

2. Use the same procedure as for your own telephone, but add the associate's name before your own. For example, "Hello, Joan Grant's office, this is Milly Reddy speaking." This lets callers know that they have reached the right office but not the expected party.

3. Offer only very limited explanations of why you are answering, rather than your associate.

4. Give the caller as many options (dealing with you, leaving a message, calling back later, etc.) as you can.

5. Avoid getting into private matters between the caller and your associate. If the caller begins to tell you more than you want or need to know, break into the flow with a request that she please wait until the associate is available.

Telephone Etiquette for the Receptionist

If you are the receptionist for your company, your role is extremely important. You represent the whole company to the caller. Your attitude determines whether a positive or negative business relationship is established between the caller and the company.

- Calls should be picked up before the third ring.

- Stay current with changes in personnel and organizational structure so that calls are properly directed.

- A pleasant, friendly tone will start the call off on the right foot.

- Chewing gum, smoking, and eating or drinking while telephoning is unprofessional.

- Music or other background noise should be at a minimum.

- If you have to perform other tasks while speaking, let the caller know. For example, "I am bringing up their extension number" or "I am ringing their pager number."

- Some companies have music or product information playing while callers are holding. This policy may be outside your control, but if you receive complaints about your particular system, you should pass the information along to a supervisor. It may be harming your company by offending callers.

- Receptionists do not need to identify themselves to callers; the company name is all that is required. It is better not to identify, unless it is necessary to have callers explain their reason for calling to reception before being redirected. Once again, this depends on the organization, but it is annoying for callers to have to explain their problem over and over again before reaching someone who can actually handle it.

- Give options for leaving messages to callers who are unable to reach their party and return to reception.

- Messages left with a receptionist should be delivered promptly. They should include time and date of the call, caller's name and number, and any message content that the caller asked to be passed on. It may also be helpful to include some extra information, such as "caller seemed worried," "irate caller," or "they said it was not urgent."

- The first caller has priority. All callers should be asked permission before being placed on hold.

- Ask for permission to answer a call when dealing with a person at the desk.

- Always call back promptly if the caller has requested this after calling when you were busy with someone else.

- A pleasant closing phrase, such as "Thank you for calling," is preferable to the ubiquitous "Have a nice day," which is suffering from severe overuse.

> **The appropriate farewell in business is "goodbye."**
> **"Bye," "So long," or "See you" are too casual.**

Telecommunication Techniques

Because of the increasing complexity of telecommunications in general, it is difficult to talk about the old style handheld telephone in isolation from other types of electronic communication devices. Many magazine articles and chat-room discussions hash over the incredibly impolite ways some people are finding to misuse electronic communication equipment. These problems range from insensitivity to abuse, from annoying to criminally irresponsible. Misuse that is seriously damaging to others may well result in the abused person seeking redress from the law. The annoying and insensitive problems will quite probably be handled in time as social mores and etiquette teach what is and what is not acceptable. These guidelines are gradually being developed, but just as the technology is new, so the manners are new and have to be learned by everyone involved.

Fifteen Problems That Underlie the Emergence of Needed Telecommunications Etiquette Guidelines

1. Pager and cell phone use in restaurants, meetings, etc. are annoying to others and prevent them from enjoying the social occasion or hearing the speakers or performers. Respect social boundaries and spaces and the rule that it is rude to interrupt.

2. Confidential messages being transmitted via a speakerphone lead to embarrassing or damaging breaches of confidentiality. Inform people of the capabilities and risks involved in the communication technology being used.

3. Unsolicited advertising faxes waste paper and tie up equipment needed for important messages. Do not impose costs on an organization for communications they are unaware of or cannot control.

4. Sending out inaccurate descriptions of a product via the Internet leads to dissatisfied customers being unwilling to risk online trade again. Do not deceive, misinform or misrepresent yourself or your company.

5. Sending on private e-mails to other addresses lead to people receiving messages not meant for their eyes. Respect confidentiality; do not send on indiscriminantly.

6. Mix-ups in e-mail addresses or telephone messages lead to personal information going astray. Use communication technologies in ways that respect the intentions of the communicator(s). Do not use or peruse communications sent to you erroneously, beyond what is required to identify the mistake.

7. Copyright infringement by people who consider all of a correspondence as belonging only to them because they initiated it. Those who are a party to them jointly own communications.

8. Videotaping or audiotaping people without their knowledge and then sharing the tapes with others. Communications should not be recorded without the knowledge and consent of all parties involved.

9. Altering taped conversations or e-mails to misrepresent what really took place. If a consensual record is made, it should be accurate and unedited.

10. Feeling obliged to answer stacks of unsolicited messages. The recipient who possesses technologies such as phone, fax or computer invites communication just as anyone with a mailbox invites mail. The recipient is under no obligation to sustain or respond to it once it has been determined to be unwanted.

11. Angry and abusive senders who resent and sometimes seek revenge for unanswered messages. The initiator of the communication must respect the recipient's desire not to sustain the communication.

12. Recipients who call back all automatically recorded numbers even though the caller did not leave a message. An unsuccessful effort to reach another party carries no obligation to leave a record of the attempt.

13. Cell phone users ask fellow diners to stop talking while answering cell phones. Request permission of those present to engage in a conversation that they are not a direct party to (e.g., use of a car phone with a passenger present).

14. Putting people on hold to answer a second caller, especially after initiating the first call. Request permission and apologize for interrupting (leaving) a communication. Return to the first caller immediately.

15. Abusive language, e-mails all in capitals. Communicate politely and in good taste.

Note: These principles are offered as sensible guidelines, rather than as rigid rules. How they can be applied in different contexts is an important research task. Given the rapidity of change and the immense variability in communication contexts, application of these guidelines is hardly automatic. There are no universal rules. Traditionally, work contexts are a little different from those in the home.

Looking back over the listed guidelines, you can quickly see that it is important to consider the feelings of the person on the other end of our communication line and to expect similar consideration in return.

Summary

- Brief announcements on automated answering systems are best. Clever, witty announcements are fun, but people have been known to call and tie up equipment just to hear the latest catchy announcement. If the space for leaving a message is brief, then the announcement should say so. Time-limited message spaces can be self-defeating if the caller redials and waits throughout your announcement a half-dozen times in order to leave a longer message anyway.

- When leaving messages, we need to be brief and remember that such messages are not always private. You cannot be certain that the one you wanted to speak to will be the only one to hear what you have taped.

- We should get permission before doing something that may make the other person uneasy, such as asking her to hold or allowing us to use a speakerphone. It is imperative to get permission when we want to tape calls.

- We need to consider the feelings of others present when we are obliged to interrupt them to take a call. We are essentially infringing on their time and making them party to information they neither need nor want.

- We must not infringe upon the privacy of others, cause them unnecessary expense, or tie up their equipment for no good reason.

- Telecommunications is a rapidly evolving field. Manners and social norms take quite a long time to develop and become established. If you do not know exactly how to behave, then remembering to treat others with respect and the same consideration for their rights as you wish shown toward yours is the best guideline for your behavior.

During the next week, become aware of how people are using telecommunications around you.

- Note where and when cell phones are being used.

- Note who your callers are and how far away they are geographically.

- Note how you answer your telephone.

- Note how others answer the phone when you call them.

- Note any annoyances with telephone communication.

Think back to a telephone communication that was less than satisfactory for you. What were the elements that caused you to be dissatisfied?

Reflections

7 NONVERBAL COMMUNICATION

The larger part of our communication is not through the words that we use but by nonverbal means. Attitude, emotions, moods, demeanor, self-worth, ability and even our personality affect and are conveyed by our stance, attire, expression, gestures and tone. The effect we have on others, both during those all-important first few seconds at introduction and later as our relationship evolves, is determined to an overwhelming extent by nonverbal communication methods.

It is difficult to assess yourself in this area. Seeing a video of yourself can help you realize where problems lie and can help make you aware that things you do are having a negative impact on others. A good friend or a business coach or mentor will also be very helpful in correcting problems. However, style and individuality are very subjective matters. No one is pleasing to or makes a good impression on everyone all the time. Striving to meet some externally imposed, "ideal businessperson" standard can result in a bland or phony image being assumed by a person who was quite acceptable before the makeover.

An honest, open, relaxed style that shows a willingness to listen and learn is a good goal to aim for.

Remember, we do not all "read" nonverbal indicators in the same way, but there are some signals that nearly everyone will interpret similarly.

For example:

- Slumped posture, folded arms and reluctant eye contact usually suggest a lack of self-confidence.

- A firm handshake tends to lead people to trust you.

- A warm, not-too-toothy smile usually gets a friendly response.

Quite often the difference between good and bad reactions to body language depends on the degree or intensity of the activity. Eye contact is essential to assuring the other party that we are paying attention to what he says. Eye contact that is too intent, however, will make us uneasy. We feel we are being interrogated, trapped or that the watcher is waiting to pounce. Some cultures dislike eye contact. For example, many Chinese people may avoid making eye contact because they consider it ill-mannered.

Things that we do unconsciously, such as habits and mannerisms, may be sending messages we do not intend. Tapping a pencil or doodling may indicate to others that we are bored, although we may not even know we are doing it while we listen carefully.

Some men automatically sit on the phone with an ankle propped on the opposite knee, leaning back, hands linked behind their head, phone jammed between ear and shoulder, with elbows out. They are relaxed and comfortable inside, but an onlooker may think they are goofing off, chatting to a friend rather than a valued client.

Someone with a poor memory for faces may scrutinize others very closely, trying to establish visual clues that will help him recall the individual when next they meet. The other party may get a different message, anything from inappropriate sexual interest to wondering if she has spinach in her teeth.

Empathy, or understanding how others feel and making an appropriate response, is now seen as a major skill for business leaders. The ability to read nonverbal messages accurately and send effective nonverbal messages to others enhances an individual's empathetic skill.

In the old style of leadership, the onus was all on the subservient party to show his position by the proper nonverbal signs. Today's leaders are more aware of their own need to send clear nonverbal messages themselves and to make an effort to understand the nonverbal messages that they receive accurately.

However, when making business contacts or when being interviewed for a job, it is still worthwhile to remember that it is up to you to make a good first impression and then maintain it by paying attention to the nonverbal messages you are sending constantly to those around you.

Attitude

Your own attitude will greatly affect the nonverbal message that you send. A positive attitude will help your posture, expression, tone and ease of movement. A good attitude can even help you:

- Seem better looking.

- Appear confident when you are not.

- Choose more appealing clothes from your closet.

- Move with greater relaxed ease.

Gestures or body language that run contrary to what is being said with the mouth are very confusing to others. Surprisingly enough people tend to believe the body language before the words just about 100 percent of the time. Telling someone you are listening while your eyes constantly stray to look at a television screen, for example, will soon have the other party convinced that you are not hearing a word he says.

> **"The right suit won't get you into the board room, but the wrong one will keep you out."**
>
> *Clothing Manufacturer's Ad*

A Word of Warning!

A negative attitude can make you:

- Less good looking.

- Seem less confident even when you are not.

- Choose less attractive clothes from your closet.

- Look uneasy.

Summary

- People who are good at reading body language are usually empathetic. They use messages they see to help understand what makes the other person tick. People may even go so far as to adjust their own behavior in response to nonverbal messages from others.

- Getting help from a trusted friend to correct negative nonverbal actions that you are sending out unwittingly to others is a sensible coping strategy.

- Do not be dismayed by seeing yourself on video for the first time. Almost everyone (even movie stars) hates looking at himself on screen.

- Don't try to fix all your bad habits at once. Fix one at a time, and give yourself lots of encouragement. It takes at least a month to form or break a habit, and even then you cannot expect to put it right first time, every time.

- "Know yourself" is good advice. For example: If you know you do not have naturally excellent taste in clothes, get help. A reputable store, where you can become an established customer, may often provide good help. They will call you when things you might find useful come in or when there is a sale on brands you prefer. Larger stores have consultants to help you make good choices. If you feel you cannot afford these options yet, shop with a good friend who knows what looks good on you.

- Business magazines will also provide good information on what the well-dressed executive is wearing. It's fun to keep up to date with fashion but beware of fads and extremes, clothes (especially shoes) that do not fit well, and anything that is very hard to keep clean.

Some Companies Will Actually Help Their Employees "Dress for Success"

If image is especially important to your organization, it may be part of the orientation process to ensure that the new employee fits the company look. Many organizations, while not going quite that far, have dress codes which make it easier to know exactly what is expected for work wear. A uniform or identifying clothing of some kind is mandatory in many industries.

Casual Days

Some companies even have a "uniform" casual-day outfit for employees to wear. About half of U.S. companies have casual days, allowing employees to wear something other than business clothing. The number of days per year when casual clothes may be worn by some employees range from occasional, to just for charitable events, to every day of the year. As with forms of address, we tend to be getting less formal in our choice of clothes for business in the U.S. When in doubt, or when entering a new situation, more conservative is a safer choice, especially for junior staff people starting their careers.

Trends Change

According to the latest surveys as reported on several women's Internet sites, there seems to be a revolt among some top women executives in larger cities such as New York and Los Angeles against the dark business suit and low-heeled shoes of the latter part of the 20th century. Very feminine clothing and high heels are making a comeback. This is happening among the topmost echelons of female executives. It may spread down to other ranks in time since fashion is constantly changing, even in the world of business.

Interview Wear Is Especially Important

The interview process may well include an assessment of how a prospective employee blends in or complements others in the department. If you are going to be interviewed by any of the larger companies, and even some of the more progressive smaller ones, you will find it worthwhile to do some research beforehand. Discover what the customary office wear is. Does the company value social interaction between employees? Does the company appreciate individuality or prefer a more conservative, homogeneous look? An ability to assess what is expected will help you prove to that company that you can become a part of its organization.

Eight Unofficial Reasons for Failing an Interview

1. Glasses hanging on a chain around the neck, which became tangled with a necklace and lapel pin when the interviewer asked for something to be read.

2. High-top sneakers were worn with a blue business suit, white shirt and striped tie.

3. Dropped a large briefcase full of books and papers in the hallway.

4. Remained seated while a staff person attempted to open a door with arms full of files.

5. Wore a very short, floral-patterned summer dress with laced, black knee-high boots.

6. Tracked snow and mud from outside into the board room.

7. Ate duck a l'orange with his hands.

8. Put salt on his food before tasting it.

These, plus many, many more examples show how important etiquette is to getting where you want to go in your career. All of the people in the list above who slipped up during their interviews had good credentials. They had the experience and skills needed to get to the interview stage. They failed to make a good impression at the interview because they did not pay attention to the importance of etiquette. There is a danger today in believing that because things are more casual and because people are more accepting of the differences and individuality of others, anything goes.

Take a closer look at the list of eight reasons why people made a poor impression.

It's easy to spot the etiquette breaches, and interesting to discover some of the conclusions that the interviewers came to about the one being interviewed.

1. Business dress should be plain with jewelry and other accessories kept to a minimum. Becoming entangled in accessories suggests this is a disorganized, unprofessional person who will keep customers waiting for answers while he tries to get things sorted out. The interviewers suspected that an untidy personal appearance suggested the candidate would have disorganized files and a messy desk.

2. Uncoordinated dress suggests an uncoordinated mind or an insufficient attention to detail. It also suggests that the person may have borrowed a business suit for the occasion and that his own clothes coordinated better with the sneakers he wore than the "suspect" suit.

3. People who carry around more than they need may be workaholics, disorganized, have poor prioritization skills or even be unable to focus on the project at hand. A briefcase that is spilled suggests that the individual may be careless with documents, allowing them to become disarranged, damaged or lost. Many companies consider workaholism a sign of a negative personality that indicates the individual will probably have problems in interpersonal relationships both in the workplace and at home.

4. This rude person would not be a valuable team player.

5. Fashion statements are fun for casual wear but not suitable for the office. The person who does not find out what is suitable to wear to work suggests to others that he makes inappropriate decisions or is a lightweight, more interested in his clothes than his job.

6. This person comes across as sloppy and uncaring.

7. Poor table manners, especially at an interview involving food, lead the interviewers to a quick conclusion that this individual will not fit in with the organization. If you are asked to a meal as part of an interview process, it is sensible to conclude that while your table manners will be under scrutiny, the interview team will also be looking at more than your choice of fork. The duck eater simply showed by his table manners that he was not management material.

8. The premature potato salter was deemed to have made an "unconsidered decision" by his rash act. Once again, the interview team was drawing some psychological conclusions from a failure to observe proper etiquette.

A Word of Warning!

Some of these examples may seem a little bizarre to you, but they are real interview incidents. Many organizations go far beyond the basic "sit across the desk and answer questions about your skills and experience" format of the past. Attention to proper etiquette, finding out what is the appropriate thing to do in a given situation and then doing it, tells the interviewer that you are a considerate, empathetic, intelligent person who wants to be accepted. Think of the impression that you want others to get from your appearance and actions and work toward that end to get the best possible results.

Presence

Some people have the ability to draw others to them, to be noticed and approved of, without any seeming effort or skill. The way they carry themselves and the energy they emit make them a focus of attention even though they are not particularly physically attractive or well-dressed.

Presence is a powerful quality, which some people have naturally.

Even if you were not born with "presence," you can develop the quality in yourself by paying attention to your attitude.

By building a positive attitude, you can improve your ability to draw others to you rather than repelling them. People with negative attitudes are repellent to others. We try to avoid those people. We do not want to socialize with them and we dread working with them. Check yourself out from time to time. Are you giving yourself negative messages that are dragging you down and building a negative attitude that puts others off?

Codes Count

Pay attention to codes of behavior if you want to be accepted in the workplace.

Every social activity has codes that make the wheels of interaction run more smoothly. It is not necessary to turn yourself into the clone of others in your department or to model yourself exactly after your mentor or coach to be accepted. However, it is important to understand that the codes of behavior, written and unspoken, are important tools to enable you to get where you want to be.

Basic Good Manners

Being polite, greeting with a friendly, open manner, helping those who need a hand, and presenting a positive attitude will all serve you well. The most important thing about good manners is that they make others feel comfortable, respected and appreciated. Thinking how you will affect others before you act is the best guide to what constitutes good manners.

- Realizing that there are people who have allergies will prevent you from making the mistake of dowsing yourself with cologne before going to the office or from smoking in the wrong place.

- Noting that there are people behind you in the buffet line will stop you from piling all the brownies onto your plate, even though they are your favorite food.

- Acknowledging that the opinions of others are as worth hearing as your own will prevent you from hogging the floor or interrupting other speakers at the meeting.

Etiquette is really a matter of common sense and giving others the respect and consideration you expect for yourself.

Try these three remedies to build a positive attitude, which will act as a magnet to draw people to you because of your "presence."

1. Recall a time when you felt great, successful and in control. Form that into a mental picture that you can recall whenever you feel yourself getting a negative feeling. Go to that place in your mind for a few seconds and let yourself experience the feeling of power, success and control again.

2. Practice walking and standing with determination and good posture. Get a friend to help you or look at a video of yourself. Slouching, slumping, hugging the walls, and shuffling are all bad habits that suggest to others that we are not worth looking at. Walking with confidence, staying alert and ready to act while sitting, a relaxed stance and open, welcoming gestures invite others to respond to your presence. Have a friend give you an honest confidence evaluation to avoid going overboard with image reform and appearing too cocky or aggressive.

3. Give yourself positive messages. Take those negative self-statements you catch yourself saying, things like, "I'm never going to get ahead," and turn them into positive self-statements, such as "I can learn to succeed" instead. Positive self-talk will help you to feel better about yourself. The choice is yours. You can believe bad things about yourself or good things. Decide to believe good things, and others will start agreeing with you.

Reflections

Body Language Exercise

Imagine yourself in the following situations and jot down your reactions:

1. A person makes too much eye contact.

2. A person avoids looking you in the eye while making conversation.

3. A person glances from your eyes to your mouth and back while you're talking.

4. A person taps a pencil while you're talking.

5. A woman crosses and uncrosses her legs while sitting.

6. A person crosses his arms after a question is asked.

7. A person sighs frequently.

8. A man looks a woman over from head to toe.

9. A person nods at you while you're talking but is looking at someone else in the room.

10. A person is doodling on a notepad while you're talking.

Reflections

Possible Responses

1. Uncomfortable, trapped, being interrogated.

2. Person is hiding the truth, is evasive.

3. A sexual message.

4. Impatient.

5. Nervous, sexual message.

6. Angry, disagreeing, defensive.

7. Bored, tired, annoyed.

8. A sexual message.

9. Not paying attention.

10. Bored, distracted.

Reflections

8 TABLE MANNERS

"Charlie, Charlie, if you're able,
Take your elbows off the table."

Why are good table manners in decline?

- Families rarely dine together in a formal setting these days.

- Family elders, such as grandparents, are not so concerned with teaching children the customs and mores of past generations.

- Social rank is now based more on wealth or fame than lineage.

- The availability of a wider variety of ethnic, snack and instant foods have made eating with the hands more acceptable.

- Busy parents rely on outside agencies such as day care or schools to teach their children basic life skills that were previously taught at home.

These are some of the reasons sociologists give for a general decline in the standard of table manners that many have noted over the past 20 years or so. It is true that unless you're dining at a formal banquet, table manners are much less strict today than in previous times. However, if you do have to attend a very formal dinner or if your business will involve foreign travel, it is still important to get informed about what will be expected of you at the table. It is very easy to give offense while dining abroad.

For most other business dining occasions, a more relaxed approach is possible as long as some basic rules are followed. Simply keep in mind the underlying purpose of good table manners, which is to eat without putting others off their food.

> **The cardinal rule to remember when business and dining coincide is that the business is more important than the food.**

Remember, especially if you are in an interview situation, trying to impress a new client or entertaining a customer, you are not there primarily to eat. Follow the lead of your host when she indicates where to sit, when to unfold your napkin, when to start eating, what to drink, and when to push back from the table. Memorizing some basic do's and don'ts will enable you to get through a business dining event with grace and the minimum of indigestion.

A good host will provide leadership while observing the guests to ensure that everyone is comfortable and well-served.

Some Table Manner Do's

- When faced with an assortment of flatware on either side of your plate, the best rule of thumb is to start with the cutlery farthest away from your plate and work in, using fresh items for each course. For example, the soup course would use the outside spoon on the right side, and the salad course would use the outside fork on the left side.

- Select foods that are easy to eat, that you enjoy and that are not the most expensive items on the menu. If you don't understand what is written on the menu, ask the server to explain what it is. Do not just order the same as your host because you can't read the menu.

- Use either the American or English style of using your knife and fork consistently throughout the meal. American-style use involves cutting up some of the food, placing the knife across the top of the plate, transferring the fork and eating with it alone, tines up. English style retains both knife and fork in the same hands throughout the meal and cutting each bite as you go, pushing the food onto the fork, tines down.

- For both styles, placing the utensils side by side at the top right edge of the plate indicates to the server that you have finished. Leaving the utensils apart on the plate indicates that you have stopped eating temporarily while you are talking or sipping your drink.

- Converse on some of the topics of a general nature that we mentioned at the start of this book. Business topics are often left until the end of the meal. Following your host's lead will let you know when it is appropriate to get onto business matters.

- It is the job of the host to provide guidance to the guests and the servers. The host should see that the guests have been attended to. If there is a very distinguished guest, then she should be served first. If necessary, the host should meet with the restaurant staff before an important dinner to ensure that everything will go smoothly.

- If you are attending an important function at an unfamiliar restaurant, then it might help you feel more at ease to go there beforehand and see what it is like. Invitations to very special events usually include an indication of what should be worn, especially if it is for formal wear.

- Lunch and breakfast meetings are considered part of a business day and regular work clothing is appropriate. If the meal invitation includes some other activity, such as golf for instance, then it is appropriate to wear sports clothes to the whole occasion. A telephoned invitation to an evening meal with business on the agenda means that business wear is acceptable. Women may add some extra accessories to a business suit if they wish, but it is not necessary to change.

- Neatness, washed hands, combed hair, and refreshed makeup are necessary preparations before going to the restaurant.

- A small gift, flowers or candy are considered polite "host gifts" when invited to a lunch or dinner at someone's home. Gifts are not necessary when going to a breakfast, for coffee, afternoon tea or pre-dinner drinks.

Some Table Manner Don'ts

- Don't do anything before your host has indicated that it is all right to proceed. It is especially bad-mannered to dig in the minute your plate arrives. Wait until all have been served or until the host invites you to begin.

- Drinking too much is a big mistake. It is safest to avoid liquor, especially at lunchtime. If you do not usually drink any kind of liquor, simply order a soda or water. It is not necessary to explain why you are ordering anything. Avoid drinks that stain the lips. Milk or grape juice can leave you with a silly looking "moustache." Use a straw if you must choose something potentially messy to drink. Do not turn your glass or cup upside down to indicate you will not be drinking.

- Ordering soup if you know you slurp or ordering spaghetti if you always splash your shirt is just asking for trouble. It is also safer not to order anything you may be tempted to eat inappropriately, either with your fingers or the wrong utensil.

- Eating directly from the buffet table is a bad breach of manners. Place items on your plate and walk away from the table before eating. Overloading your plate is another no-no. A good way to stop yourself from piling on your favorite tidbits is to place your glass on your plate, only leaving a rim for food items. This also enables you to keep your right hand free for handshakes, gestures and popping the occasional canapé into your mouth.

- The food that is in your mouth should be invisible to others while you eat. Take small bites so that you can converse while eating without breaking this major rule.

- Most children learn not to put their elbows on the table. It is not permissible for grownups either, except between courses or when the meal is over. Elbows should be kept in while eating, especially at a banquet where seating can sometimes be crowded, or if you are left-handed and constantly hitting against your right-handed neighbor's arm.

- Picking up something you have dropped is the job of the server. Indicate that you have lost a utensil or your napkin and ask for a new one.

- If you must leave the table during a meal, and it is really best not to do so if possible, then you should excuse yourself to your fellow diners. It is not necessary or desirable to explain why or where you are going. Try to be as unobtrusive as possible.

- While dining, your napkin remains folded lengthwise across your lap. Put it there when your host unfolds hers. Use it during the meal to lightly blot your lips, especially if you suspect you have food around your mouth. The napkin is not there to be a bib, a handkerchief, to polish the cutlery or glasses or to mop your brow. After you are through eating, lay the napkin beside your plate. Do not refold it or lay it on top of your plate in the leftover food.

- Do not eat as if you were starving. "Leaving a little for manners" is still a good tip, but neither should you order an expensive meal and waste it. Do not ask for a doggie bag.

- Discussion of what you can and cannot eat, special diets, food allergies, diseases — especially those related to food — and food foibles that you consider ridiculous but which others present may have or any topic likely to revolt or disgust people must be avoided at the table.

- Do not pick your teeth at the table. Try to avoid touching yourself, especially your hair, nose, ears, etc. while dining. Applying makeup, combing the hair or scratching while at the table are all very bad-mannered acts.

- Any kind of bodily noise is strictly forbidden at the polite North American table. If you have to cough, sneeze or blow your nose during a meal, turn away from the table, and especially away from your neighbor's plate. If you cannot reach your handkerchief in time to smother a sneeze, then it is permissible to cover your mouth with your napkin in this emergency situation.

- Gulping your food is not a good idea. Doing so may make you belch. Eat slowly, take small bites and chew properly. This, along with not talking when your mouth is very full, will help avoid food going the wrong way, which results in embarrassing coughing fits or even choking.

- Smoking while others are eating is not permissible.

- Scolding or blaming the server for a mistake is for the host to do, if necessary, after the guests have left.

- Pushing a guest to take something they don't want is not the way for a host to make guests comfortable.

- While some American, African or Mideastern dishes are eaten with the fingers, it is fairly safe to say that using the correct utensils is the way to go when dining in most U.S. restaurants. If you are adept, then it is fine to eat with chopsticks, but if you know you are not practiced, then ask the server for a fork. It is better not to risk sending food flying into your neighbor's lap.

- Do not offer or ask to taste or share what you or your neighbor has ordered.

> "We were to do more business after dinner;
> but after dinner is after dinner — an old saying and true,
> much drinking, little thinking."
>
> *Jonathan Swift*

In-Office Eating

This has become popular in recent times. Workers will often share snacks, potluck meals or ordered-in food as part of team-building social occasions, or because a special project keeps them busy through lunch or after hours.

When dining out, the host always pays. If the group brings a meal in or lunch orders are taken, then each person pays for her own meal. If it is a morale-booster meeting with snacks or a small celebration, then the food is often paid for out of petty cash or brought in from home by the participants.

Similar guidelines apply to eating informally in the office as to eating in a dining room.

- Be neat and do not put others off by your behavior.

- Don't grab more than your fair share.

There are also specific hazards to eating at the office.

- Be careful of messy foods. Even such simple items as sugared or filled donuts may powder and splash you and others around you.

- Potlucks are fun, but avoid bringing either something really inadequate or something far too grand. A small box of doughnut holes won't go far as dessert for 20 people, but your grandmother's authentic charlotte russe in an heirloom Bavarian crystal bowl is way over the top for the monthly staff meeting.

- Paper plates and cups and plastic utensils are not as strong as metal, glass and china. Spills and upsets are easy when you are eating off your lap.

- Keep food away from important documents and sensitive electronic equipment.

- Do not go to attend to a customer or client clutching a slice of pizza, or answer the phone through a mouthful of birthday cake.

Human beings use dining as a time to extend social connections and develop relationships. In a business context, it is also used to assess others personally and, through them, the company for which they work. Presenting yourself and your company in the best light by paying attention to your table manners is good business practice in today's highly competitive world.

Practice makes perfect for table manners.

Set up your own dining table according to some of the etiquette books available today. An updated Emily Post book is an excellent source of information.

Then, practice a meal using the correct cutlery, napkin, water and wine glasses, etc.

As an alternative, take yourself to a fine-dining establishment and use your new information to deal with the formal requirements of the table service.

Reflections

A Finer-Points Quiz

1. Napkin or serviette? Which is correct?

2. What do you do if there's a small knife on the bread and butter plate?

3. What do you do if the waiter pours a small amount of wine in your wine glass?

4. On which side will the waiter serve you? Take the plates away?

5. What do you do if you spill something on the table?

6. What do you do if you know you've got some food stuck in your tooth?

7. What do you do if the waiter stands behind your chair as you are being seated?

8. What do you do if the waiter picks up your napkin?

9. How do you sip soup from a spoon?

10. What do you do with butter from the butter dish?

Reflections

Answers

1. Napkin is always correct. Serviette is usually the paper variety.

2. The small knife is for spreading butter only. Don't use it for cutting food. Leave it on the edge of the butter plate.

3. The waiter wants you to sample the wine by taking a small sip and nodding approval if you want more.

4. The waiter will serve from your left and take from your right.

5. Don't fuss. Call the waiter over. Or, if a large spill, cover discreetly with your napkin — don't blot at it.

6. Whatever you do — don't suck your teeth or use your fingers or other utensil to dislodge it. Excuse yourself and floss in the restroom.

7. The waiter is going to push your chair in for you. Stand in front of your chair and the waiter will push it forward until it touches the back of your knees. Then sit and pull it up closer if needed.

8. The waiter will put the napkin on your lap.

9. Put the spoon in the bowl and scoop away from you. Sip from the edge of the spoon.

10. Take a pat of butter and put it on the side of the bread and butter plate. Don't butter the whole slice of bread at once. Break off a bit of bread, butter it and eat it as needed.

Reflections

9 NETWORKING

In the past, "rubbing elbows" was a euphemism given to networking. People attended functions and hoped to meet people who could be helpful to them in business. They were warned about being too forward and told not to offer a business card unless the other party requested it. Networking skills are seen as a valuable asset for the businessperson. People are not coy about offering a business card as they introduce themselves. The benefits of business connections outweigh the fear of appearing pushy or aggressive.

Networking still requires that some attention be paid to the requirements of etiquette, however. It's like the old song says, "It's not what you do, but the way that you do it. That's what gets results." Using good manners will make a better impression at the time and ensure that you are remembered favorably later.

The Equality of Invitation

Attending a function gives people permission to treat each other as equals, even if they are actually not on a par, either socially or professionally. It is good manners on the part of those of higher standing to remember that fact when they attend functions such as conventions, association meetings and corporate events. People who act snobbishly to those of lower rank in any situation are displaying very bad manners.

When approaching someone of higher rank though, it is wise to be especially careful to avoid giving offense.

- Do not interrupt a conversation.

- Try to get someone to introduce you if you can.

- Remember to use the person's title and a more formal mode of address.

All those present at a function to which they have been specifically invited are expected to mingle and make themselves available to talk to everyone else.

Seven Tips for Making a Favorable First Impression Last

1. Keep the initial encounter short. A 10- to 15-minute conversation is usually ample for an introductory meeting.

2. Use the person's name at least once during the conversation.

3. Use body-language signals that show you are listening, interested and attentive to the person. Do not let your attention wander, seeking out new people to meet.

4. If someone else joins you whom you know, then make introductions even though he may be a business competitor.

5. Use the person's name again as you shake hands and bring the meeting to a close.

6. Note one or two things that the person talked about on the back of his card as soon as you leave him.

7. Follow up with a call, e-mail or note in a couple of days if you want to take things further. Mention some of the things you talked about together. You will find it easy to keep topics and individuals sorted out if you made the notes as suggested in the previous point.

Business Cards

If you've ever had to fumble for your business card, spilling out the contents of your briefcase or purse to find it, you'll know how uncomfortable you felt. And if all you found was an old, mangled, dog-eared card at the bottom of the pile, the impression that you left with the other person was an indelible one.

Your business card represents both you and your organization to strangers. Make sure that your card expresses the kind of image you want to leave with the person you have just met. Cards that are dirty or dog-eared, tumbled with odds and ends in the bottom of a briefcase or purse, or mixed up with tissues in your pocket are not acceptable. A business card holder, readily available, is the professional way to keep cards stored neatly. Your own cards go on one side and cards you collect on the other. Transfer collected cards to your files regularly, to avoid getting overloaded.

Many people are becoming more innovative with card design now that it is possible to produce cards quickly and easily on the computer. If you want to produce your own cards, beware of leaving out important information.

A business card should contain:

1. Company name
2. Cardholder name
3. Cardholder title/function
4. Location
5. Telephone number
6. Fax number
7. E-mail address
8. Mailing address

9. Indication of the product or service offered by the organization

10. The logo or a modified version of the company logo, if possible

That's a lot of information to get onto a small card, but don't be tempted to use large or folded cards. Nonstandard cards can cause problems if they do not fit readily into other people's business card holders.

Card Etiquette

In the past, there was a very complicated system of etiquette surrounding the whole business of leaving, giving and receiving cards. Fortunately for us, this has gone by the board and today most people simply exchange cards or ask for another person's card as they please. Strictly speaking, to maintain the rules of precedence, the most important person should initiate an exchange of cards when meeting on neutral ground. The visitor offers his card when coming into a meeting on the other person's territory. It is also becoming more acceptable to exchange cards at social events. This may be partially because of relaxed rules of etiquette and also the greater emphasis on networking.

It seems that since now people of both sexes are likely to be in the work force, there is less demand for a definite separation between social and business time with business talk previously deemed taboo at the dinner table. Business is an accepted topic of conversation, and people are more accepting of the idea of following up a social contact for business purposes, in an open way.

It is only necessary to note down names and addresses and ask for an exchange of business cards later if you are at a formal function wearing evening dress or in sports clothes involved in a game. It is not considered appropriate to carry business cards at such times.

Do not include business cards in correspondence unless specifically requested to do so or unless you are sending company brochures or other printed materials. Staple or clip the card to the literature so that it is not lost.

Zippy, colorful cards with unique designs are a plus if you are a graphic designer or in the entertainment industry. Plainer, more traditional cards are probably a safer choice for most companies. Many organizations have cards printed to company specifications for their employees. If this is the case for you, then your decisions are made for you. When the choice is yours, remember that you may be stuck with your decision for a long time. Be sure that the card tells the recipient what you want them to know and remember about you when you are no longer present.

If you have both a company and a personal card, then use two holders and keep them together so that you are not scrambling through your pockets or purse for the second holder.

Summary

Business cards are important details in today's world of business networking. It is good business practice to exchange and give business cards that reflect you and your company with messages you want others to receive and retain when you are no longer present.

Take some time to sort out the business cards that you've been given. Use a Rolodex, business card box or some other holder to organize them.

Take a look at your own business cards. Are they fresh and crisp, easy to access and reflective of your professional persona?

Reflections

10 BUSINESS GIFTS

The tendency in business in the U.S. in recent years is for people to become more wary of giving and accepting business gifts. Problems with tax laws and sensitivity to questions of conflict of interest and ethics have made people cautious about accepting or offering anything that could possibly be construed as a bribe. We are also much more aware nowadays that actions that seem perfectly reasonable at present may be viewed differently at some future date.

As a result, some organizations have a strict "no-gift" policy. Others limit the value of gifts given or will only allow acceptance of items such as plaques or trophies for company achievement rather than gift items for individuals. If you wish to give a gift to a business associate, it is good policy to check with the human resources department of the company so that you do not violate such rulings.

It is also necessary to be sensitive to ethnic, religious or cultural factors when selecting a gift. For example:

- Leather articles are offensive to people of the Hindu faith.

- Clocks are considered to be unlucky gifts by many Chinese people.

- A gift of lingerie to a woman associate may well be construed as sexual harassment. Cash is always considered as a bribe when it exceeds the amount given as tips to servers.

Small gifts that reflect an individual's personal life, such as a hobby item, are the most appropriate. Flowers are now considered an appropriate gift for both men and women. Flowers, candy or wine (if you know the person reasonably well) are customary gifts to take when dining in an associate's home. If you are invited formally to a special event, it is not appropriate to bring a "host gift."

Some events, such as fund-raisers, roasts, morale boosters and in-house award ceremonies, Christmas parties, showers or team social occasions do include giving or exchanging gifts. These are often requested to be "fun gifts." Sometimes a price limit is set for office Christmas or shower gifts. Suggesting that a joint gift be given may be appropriate. If contributions are made, it is not good manners to indicate how much each person gave.

Wacky, witty "fun gifts" that fit the individual without being offensive or going overbudget are usually pretty hard to find. It is in poor taste to greatly exceed the suggested cost, as it makes others who obeyed the rules look cheap.

If you work for a large organization, it may be wise to consider a policy that allows only cards to be exchanged at work. The whole business of giving gifts to colleagues can get very cumbersome and expensive. People end up giving to associates they do not know. There is a danger of individuals being overlooked. In order to foster a more positive attitude, it may be necessary to make a realistic policy that limits gifts as a rule.

If your company has a gift-giving policy for valued customers or clients, then it is wise to keep very strictly within those guidelines and make sure that the gift is known to be from your organization and not from you personally.

Summary

It is great to receive gifts. We all enjoy being honored by our associates. It is important these days to be especially careful about giving and getting gifts. Follow company policy exactly and make sure that the gifts you select for others are truly appropriate. If your organization does not have the sort of policy it may need to meet today's gift-giving requirements, then consider raising the matter with your supervisor or human resources department.

Write **A** for Appropriate or **I** for Inappropriate next to each of these gift-giving situations.

1. Mr. Brown gives his secretary, who has been with him for 22 years, an expensive silk scarf for Christmas. _____

2. Mr. Brown gives his secretary, who has been with him for two months, an expensive silk scarf for Christmas. _____

3. Jolene gives her co-worker Cal a bottle of liquor to congratulate him for his recent promotion. _____

4. Jolene gives her co-worker Cal a funny poster to congratulate him for his recent promotion. _____

5. Henry gives his biggest client a $100 gift voucher to an exclusive men's accessories store. _____

6. Henry gives his biggest client a $100 gift voucher for the company product. _____

7. Mary gives her boss, Mr. Barnes, a subscription to *Playboy* for his birthday. _____

8. Mary gives her boss, Mr. Barnes, a subscription to *Field and Stream* for his birthday. _____

9. Tina gives her biggest client a basket of fruit for Christmas. _____

10. Tina gives her biggest client an engraved gold watch with the company logo for Christmas. _____

Reflections

Answers

1. Appropriate — they have a longstanding relationship.

2. Inappropriate — it is a personal gift and the relationship is too short for this.

3. Inappropriate — liquor is not considered a business gift.

4. Appropriate — but only if Jolene and Cal have a relationship where joking is the norm.

5. Inappropriate — it is a personal gift.

6. Appropriate — it is a business gift.

7. Inappropriate — it has sexual connotations.

8. Inappropriate — it is still a personal gift that is outside the business context.

9. Appropriate — if the company policy allows this.

10. Appropriate — if the company provides the watch and it is policy.

    Inappropriate — if Tina buys the watch.

Reflections
Reflections

11 HANDLING DIFFICULT SITUATIONS

No matter how hard we try, difficult situations and times when emotions can get out of control do happen. It is important to deal with emotional situations that arise in the workplace sensibly, quickly and with the minimum of upheaval. Keeping emotional situations as private as possible is best for morale.

The avoidance of loud, aggressive, abusive conflict and physical violence is essential. Any disciplining or negative comments that have to be made to subordinates must be carried out in private. Treat peers with respect and avoid complaining about people with whom you are having problems to others. Bona fide complaints should only be addressed to the proper superior.

Do not undermine the authority of superiors or talk about them behind their backs. If you have a problem with someone in authority, go through the appropriate channels to make a formal complaint. Have good documentation for all complaints and keep calm when going over them. Keep the issues work-centered, avoiding personalities, blaming and sweeping generalizations. Do not exaggerate problems or drag in third parties who are not really involved to back you up. Document all problem situations thoroughly with times, dates and signatures of witnesses if need be. Know your organization's structure so you approach the right person(s) if you have to take the problem higher.

Keep emotional displays, tears, yelling and physically acting out in control when dealing with difficult situations, but show sympathy and consideration for anyone who is in distress.

Sexual Harassment

Sexual harassment is a serious problem. It must be handled properly through the correct channels. Lawsuits can result if abusive behavior goes unchecked. Harassing behavior seldom affects just one victim. Good documentation and swift action are essential.

Anger

Know your hot buttons (what makes you angry or lose control) and practice keeping them switched off. Knowing the sore spots that trigger an emotional reaction on your part will help you maintain better control and keep a sense of proportion when things go wrong. Have a buddy outside the office to sound off to about persistent problems.

Root Out Root Causes

Be fair. There are two sides to every argument. Listening and asking open-ended questions will help to clarify the real cause of problems. It is more effective to find out the real cause and properly address the true situation than to keep fixing what you think is going wrong and then discover it was not the root problem.

Don't Lose Your Sense of Humor

The ability to laugh at yourself is one of your strongest coping mechanisms for handling difficult situations.

Remember: A friendly, open attitude to others will usually be reciprocated. Snobbishness, trying to look superior to peers, a know-it-all attitude, fawning on those in higher positions and rudeness to those lower on the corporate ladder leave you vulnerable to displays of resentment and animosity.

Summary

- Protect yourself and others by careful attention to documentation of problems that arise in the workplace.

- Romantic relationships in the workplace are very difficult to handle. It is best to avoid them totally.

- Never correct or discipline subordinates in front of others.

- Listening carefully and handling problems promptly and fairly prevent negative attitudes and resentment from building up in the workplace.

Think of a situation that is causing you some emotional concern right now.

Ask yourself these questions:

1. Who are the players in this situation?

2. What are the stakes?

3. What is my position in regard to status/authority?

4. What do I stand to gain if I confront the situation?

5. What do I stand to lose if I don't?

6. Who else will stand by me?

7. Have any of my "hot buttons" been pushed in this situation?

8. What is my best course of action?

Reflections

12 MEETINGS

> **"A meeting is a place where minutes are kept
> and hours are wasted."**

Studies show that middle managers are spending up to 25 percent to 39 percent of their time in meetings. Yet everyone in business complains about the waste of time so many meetings represent. Meetings are also fertile ground for negativity to grow in. To counter some of the bad aspects of meetings, many organizations have begun establishing rules regulating the calling of meetings, and establishing etiquette guidelines for those attending.

For example:

- There must be a clearly stated reason or purpose for the meeting to be called.

- Unnecessary meetings must be cancelled.

- Meetings are not to be held simply because they are established traditionally.

- Meetings are not for giving someone a captive audience.

- Meetings are not to be called merely as fronts for socializing.

- Meetings must be truly participatory, not to provide a seemingly democratic veneer to hide dictatorial leadership.

These regulations prevent some of the major time-wasting aspects of unnecessary meetings. They go some way toward ensuring that others are treated with consideration and respect.

Some more good rules to follow once the meeting has been called will go even further toward ensuring that meetings do not infringe upon the rights of those who attend.

For example:

- Do not include people who do not need to attend.

- Start and end on time.

- Have an agenda and stick to it.

- Make sure everyone knows the purpose, goals and objectives of the meeting.

- Allow for reasonable input and curtail unreasonable input.

- Notify those who are taking part in the meeting ahead of time and warn them if they are expected to contribute, bring information or make a report.

- Deal with important items first.

- The chairperson is like the host. She is expected to be in control of the meeting.

Individual chairpersons may institute rules to combat particular problems of etiquette, especially if some participants are often rude or inconsiderate.

Negative attitudes that threaten good teamwork may make establishing these rules vital.

For example:

- No interrupting another speaker.

- No criticism of another's ideas without a positive suggestion of one's own.

- Attendees must be on time and remain for the whole meeting.

- No shouting.

While these seem like very basic examples of everyday good manners that most people learn in grade school or earlier, it has been found necessary by some companies to enforce such rules to enable teams to work together and meet without discord.

Five Most Commonly Heard Complaints About Bad Manners in Meetings

1. Hogging the floor

2. Ineffective leadership

3. Awkward timing

4. Going over schedule

5. Not listening

Suggestions

The one time it is not bad manners to interrupt is when someone is being too long-winded — taking more than her fair share of time at a meeting to put forth her point of view. Such people are guilty of a blatant disregard for the feelings of the poor trapped listener(s). It is therefore quite acceptable to interrupt them and end their inappropriate behavior. The effective chairperson will do so in a quiet, polite, firm way that leaves no room for equivocation.

Strong leadership by a chairperson who is considerate of others is key to holding a successful meeting. Making sure that the agenda is followed is part of that strong leadership. Assertive leaders will probably also be aware of problems of timing for those in attendance; they should be willing to make compromises so that everyone can attend with as much ease as possible.

Meetings that pretend to be opportunities for input from everyone, but where the decisions have already been made, are a farce. They make everyone attending disgruntled and cynical. It is better to stick with a traditional, hierarchical style for the organization than to use meetings to create a false appearance of a consensual format.

Location

It is part of the duties of the one who calls the meeting to ensure that there is a proper place for people to congregate.

If the meeting is official, arrangements for taking minutes and serving refreshments should be made before the meeting starts. Less formal meetings should have a roster system for any necessary tasks, and this system should include all those who attend.

Just because the meeting is informal or only made up of co-workers does not mean good manners do not apply.

Visitors

If visitors are attending a meeting in your office, then having them escorted to your door is a nice touch. Letting the receptionist know that you expect a visitor will also denote that the visitor is valued and that you are prepared to receive them. If you are running late, make sure the visitor is told and asked if she would mind waiting for a few moments (in a comfortable holding area if possible). Lead the visitor to your office and have her precede you inside. Take her coat and hang it neatly. Indicate where the visitor should sit.

Interruptions

Do not allow calls to interrupt meetings that have been made by appointment. If you are visiting someone and she takes a call, tell her that you will reschedule and leave.

Escort Visitors Out

When the meeting is over, either escort the visitor to the door yourself or call for someone to take her out.

Rules of Order

Large meetings with attendees who do not all know one another do not necessitate long introductions. The chairperson should provide copies of the agenda and a roster of attendees for everyone. Robert's Rules of Order are almost always followed at formal meetings. A good chairperson is familiar with the rules of order and applies them fairly.

Ensure the Comfort of Those in Attendance

Designated seating with place names is a good way of having everyone know who is attending. Equipping the room with writing materials and basic refreshments such as water and mints is a good way of showing that you care about the comfort of the participants. Reasonably comfortable seating, a table to write on, good lighting and sound, a bearable temperature and good ventilation are all helpful for ensuring the satisfaction of meeting participants.

Empathize. Participants will show by their body language when they are "all meetinged out." Exhausted, angry, resentful people are not usually very productive. If you have underestimated the time needed, then break off the meeting and table the rest of the agenda to another time.

Confirming Prevents Slip-Ups

Confirm meeting or any appointment times beforehand. If the meeting is early in the day, confirm the day before. Monday morning appointments should be confirmed on Friday, or those after a holiday, before it. Afternoon appointments and meetings can be confirmed the morning of the same day, unless they are at a distance.

Escorting

The person who greets you and leads you to an appointment should go ahead regardless of gender. If that person is not your host, then thank her before greeting your host. Do not remove outdoor clothing or take a seat in another person's office until invited to do so.

It is a nice touch to send a handwritten note of thanks after a meeting or appointment that you have requested. Thanking the person for her time, letting her know that you valued her input and that you hope to meet again will leave a favorable impression.

A Word of Warning!

We sometimes think it necessary only to thank others when things go well for ourselves. Even if that appointment did not turn out to be as fruitful as you hoped, the thank-you note is still good etiquette.

A thank-you note is also a precautionary measure. Things change in business. You may need to approach that person again in the future. You may even find yourself asking her for a job one day. Attention to the niceties today will likely stand you in good stead tomorrow. Besides, forming good manners takes practice. The more you use proper etiquette, the more it will become second nature to do so.

Self-Assessment Survey

How do you handle meetings? Fill in each question blank with one of the following:

O — Often

S — Seldom

N — Never

1. I send both meeting announcements and agenda surveys to participants well in advance. _____

2. I ask for attendance confirmation and/or make reminder memos or calls prior to the meeting day. _____

3. I arrange documentation for the meeting well in advance. _____

4. I prepare materials for the meeting well in advance. _____

5. I listen without interrupting when someone is speaking. _____

Reflections

13 MENTORS AND MENTORING

Many of the top business executives today will tell you frankly that they owe at least part of their success to the help they got early in their careers from a good mentor. A mentor is a more experienced person who encourages and assists those starting out on their career paths. Although some career advisors recommend having a mentor of the same sex, gender should not be an issue in a successful mentoring relationship.

In the past, the ball was always in the mentor's court when it came to selecting the one to be mentored. An ambitious youngster would hope to catch the eye of someone in authority to take him under his wing and help him to advance. Nowadays the enterprising newcomer is more likely to seek out and request mentoring from a senior person who seems likely. If you know someone in your organization whom you could persuade to help you advance, go ahead and make the approach yourself.

Of course, you will need to make a favorable impression. You must be polite and temper your enthusiasm to suit your audience. You will, since the request is so much more important to you than to the mentor, need to use empathy to let the mentor know there are some advantages for him in the process.

People become mentors for many reasons.

- They may want to have an heir to carry on their ideas and projects after they retire.

- They may enjoy teaching and training and have little other opportunity to practice their skills.

- They may want to keep channels open to the shop floor or front desk through the one they mentor.

- Perhaps they just enjoy the enthusiasm and fresh ideas that young people bring.

When you approach a prospective mentor, be honest about what you hope the mentor will do for you, but also let the mentor know that you want to be helpful to him too. Spend some time finding a mentor who is active and in the swim. Some senior executives have simply been kicked upstairs and have little real power or business acumen. Look for a mentor whose ideas mesh well with your own. It is not helpful to you if the mentor's advice is to do just the opposite of what you want to do. Nor is it polite to ask for advice and then not take it. It is not at all appropriate to "buy" a mentor with gifts, but if a mentor has helped you in a specific situation, then a handwritten note of thanks must be sent.

For example:

You are invited to a lunch meeting with several senior executives. You know that this is probably the meeting that will make or break your try for promotion to assistant head of the department. You talk to your mentor about the invitation and ask for tips. Thanks to those tips, you are able to study up on your host's favorite hobby, you steer clear of mentioning football, which he hates, and you are able to give an informed opinion about sales projections for the upcoming year.

Send a note of thanks immediately after the meeting to let your mentor know that things seemed to go well because you were able to use the helpful information you were given. A small gift such as flowers could also be sent, depending on the individual. Your mentor should be the first to know if your promotion comes through.

Taking a mentor out for a meal or coffee is also a nice gesture. It is customary at in-house business dining situations for the most senior executive to play host and pick up the tab. Returning the favor for a mentor, even though he is probably in a much higher salary bracket than you, is a sign that you not only appreciate the help he gives, but also that you want to repay his generosity in some measure. Playing the host for your mentor will also help you to practice your social skills on a friendly audience.

Ask for helpful criticism from your mentor in as many different business situations as possible.

Multiple Mentors

In some cases it is necessary to have more than one guide. A mentor who can help you develop technical skills or meet clients may be useful when you are learning your profession. A mentor who is socially and/or politically astute within the organization will be more helpful as your career path moves into management areas.

It is very impolite to dump a past mentor. It is not astute, either. People who have been strong enough to help you climb the ladder of success are almost certainly strong enough to pull you down again if you give them cause to regret the assistance they gave. Although you may no longer have as much contact with previous mentors as your career develops, keeping in touch, continuing to thank them and acknowledging the help they gave are proper courses of action.

It is also good to continue the process. Introduce a promising newcomer to your first mentor and become a part of succession planning for your organization.

Become a Mentor Yourself

Not everyone has the requisite skills for being an effective mentor. Learning those skills can give your career an interesting new dimension. You do not have to be an elder statesman to be a mentor. Cooperation and teamwork are more than just buzzwords in today's business scene. Mentoring skills can be developed and are useful in building strong teams, forming cohesive work groups, diminishing divisive interdepartmental competition, and keeping everybody on the side of company goals and objectives. There are codes of etiquette for both the mentor and the protégé to follow that will help the system work well.

Good Advice for the Mentor

- Be honest and give constructive criticism.

- Do not choose someone to mentor only because you want an ally or simply to push your own agenda.

- Have a genuine liking for the one you mentor.

- Make sure that the one you mentor really does share your goals and values.

- Keep the relationship on a business level. Avoid becoming too closely involved in the personal life of the one you mentor and especially avoid any suggestion of a sexual liaison.

> **"By definition, mentoring is a relational experience whereby one person shares information with another. The mentor must be willing to invest his life in the life of the person being mentored."**
>
> *Joe Gilliam*

Summary

- Mentors will select people who are ambitious, energetic, intelligent and personable. You can influence a mentor to take you on by showing him that you are a worthwhile candidate for promotion, that you fit the organization, and that you are willing to learn.

- Good mentors help their protégés grow by delegating tasks, giving advice and improving opportunities to network with those who will help advancement.

- Know-it-all types, controllers, workaholics and people with low self-esteem and/or insecurities make poor mentors. It pays to look around carefully before approaching someone to be your mentor.

- Shared values are vital to the well-being of any relationship. Politics, religion, gender, age and status can all influence the relationship, but disparate life values will undermine relationships quicker than any other factor.

- Mentoring often involves knowing something about what drives the other person. Dreams, visions, hopes and goals are very personal things. Make sure that your mentor is one who will respect your confidences and deal honestly with your aims and ambitions.

- A good mentoring relationship has clearly defined boundaries. Protégés should not telephone the mentor at home or try to become friends with members of the mentor's family.

- The protégé should not visit the mentor's home without a specific invitation.

- Cards or gifts should not be sent to the mentor's home except in cases of serious illness or bereavement or unless the protégé has been formally invited to a social event by the mentor.

- The protégé should value the mentor's time as if it were his own and restrict office visits to suit the mentor.

- At the start of a mentoring relationship, the mentor should initiate all meetings. If the protégé feels the need of emergency assistance, then it is polite to call and make an appointment for when the mentor is free to converse.

Think of the people that you know both inside and outside of your organization.

1. Who would make a good mentor for you?

2. What information do they have that would benefit you?

3. How could you approach them to be your mentor?

4. What would they get out of mentoring you?

Reflections

14 A FINAL WORD

This book has been written to help you avoid some of the pitfalls that you may encounter as you move forward in your career. There is a tendency today to believe that etiquette, politeness and good manners are not as important as they were in the past. While it is true that many of the rigid codes that once governed all social and business activity have vanished, it is still very important to behave correctly in certain circumstances. It is also helpful and pleasant to behave correctly in general.

It Makes Good Sense to Develop Your Social Skills

At a time when many organizations are moving toward cooperative, consensual relational structure, it makes sense to develop the social skills that improve your ability to work well with others at every level.

There is also a noticeable tendency toward improving customer service, both within and without the organization. The polite person with basic good manners is bound to make a better impression on customers.

Practicing good business etiquette then makes sense in the highly competitive world of today. Those who want to get ahead will learn how to help themselves by acting properly in all business situations. Think of your present work situation and imagine how a firm grasp of what constitutes good business etiquette will help you to advance.

Peers appreciate working with a cheerful, cooperative co-worker, one who greets them with a smile, deals with problems quietly and does not hold a grudge. Your friendly attitude and self-confidence will help them accept you as a supervisor when you are promoted. They will agree that you have earned your promotion and are likely to provide good leadership.

Subordinates who work for you, or those on your team who are directed by you, feel confident that you will provide fair, consistent, considerate leadership. Your self-confidence, knowledge and willingness to listen and take advice motivate your workers. You are ready to share responsibility, train and delegate. Quick with deserved thanks and praise, you never pass off the achievements of others as your own. You encourage others to participate fully in production and are open to learning from those who are on the front line. You remain on friendly terms with those who were your peers but do not show favoritism. When a crisis hits, you are willing to roll up your sleeves and help get the job done.

Superiors are willing to promote you, not just because you are good at your job, but also because you have made an effort to understand the vision, purpose and structure of the organization. You take steps to learn and develop the new skills needed as your career progresses. You are a credit to the organization, and those in upper management are not ashamed to have you on their side when dealing with customers and clients outside the company. Your business or professional skills are good, but you also realize that there are important social skills needed to succeed in upper management. Your attention to detail, networking skills and willingness to listen and learn from others will make you a good representative of your company at conventions, meetings with sister companies, at the head office, or even on trips overseas.

Mentors spot your enthusiasm and willingness to learn, and select you as a person worth investing in for the future of the company. You are able to take criticism and evaluation constructively, using them as tools to help you grow your skills and learn new ways to advance. A neat, well-groomed appearance and attention to the office dress code make it easy for the mentor to introduce you to her associates. You are willing to take the advice of the mentor and show proper gratitude for the assistance you are given.

Customers and clients enjoy doing business with you. You know your job and do it well, but you are also a pleasant person to meet. You listen and take the time for the small personal touches that round out a business relationship and make people want to come back to do business with you again. Your communication style is considerate, clear and polite. Meeting with you in the office or going out for a meal is a pleasure. You never miss appointments, mix up dates, make unrealistic promises, boast about your successes, put down competitors, waste time with boring anecdotes or embarrass people by telling inappropriate jokes. They appreciate your habit of sending a handwritten card to mark special occasions.

Etiquette Is Never Out of Style

Etiquette is important in every aspect of business life. It is the essential oil that keeps the wheels of our societal systems functioning smoothly. Far from being something you can ignore, etiquette remains a hot issue. All major business magazines have a business-etiquette column, and most issues contain letters with questions about business do's and don'ts that trouble the readers.

The Internet abounds with information about the pitfalls associated with poor business etiquette. The development of rules of behavior governing use of electronic communications is a primary concern for responsible users, especially those who are aware of how strongly many people feel about their increasing usage in our modern world.

Rapid changes in technical development may mean that an etiquette governing usage is playing catch-up in finding acceptable coping strategies, but it does not mean that people are willing to ignore the need for those strategies to exist.

Be a Lifelong Learner

As always, the best advice to those who would succeed at any task is to keep learning. Subscribe to a reputable business magazine or visit an Internet chat room to keep up-to-date on new developments. If you really want to grow your career, then learning what it takes in all aspects and at every level is your best strategy for success.

INDEX

Buy any 3, get 1 FREE!

Get a 60-Minute Training Series™ Handbook FREE ($14.95 value)*
when you buy any three. See back of order form for full selection of titles.

These are helpful how-to books for you, your employees and co-workers. Add to
your library. Use for new-employee training, brown-bag seminars, promotion gifts and
more. Choose from many popular titles on a variety of lifestyle, communication, productivity
and leadership topics. Exclusively from National Press Publications.

BUY 3 GET 1 FREE! Buy more, save more

DESKTOP HANDBOOK ORDER FORM

Ordering is easy:

1. Complete both sides of this Order Form, detach, and mail, fax or phone your order to:

    Mail: National Press Publications
                   P.O. Box 41907
                   Kansas City, MO 64141-6107

    Fax: 1-913-432-0824
    Phone: 1-800-258-7248 (in Canada 1-800-685-4142)
    Internet: http://www.natsem.com/books.html

2. Please print:

    Name_____ Position/Title _____

    Company/Organization_____

    Address_____City _____

    State/Province_____ZIP/Postal Code _____

    Telephone (____)_____ Fax (____) _____

3. Easy payment:

    ❏ Enclosed is my check or money order for $_____ (total from back).
    Please make payable to National Press Publications.

    Please charge to:
    ❏ MasterCard   ❏ VISA   ❏ American Express

    Credit Card No. _____ Exp. Date_____

    Signature_____

• •

MORE WAYS TO SAVE:

SAVE 33%!!! BUY 20-50 COPIES of any title ... pay just $9.95 each ($11.25 Canadian).

SAVE 40%!!! BUY 51 COPIES OR MORE of any title ... pay just $8.95 each ($10.25 Canadian).

* $17.00 in Canada

60-MINUTE TRAINING SERIES™ HANDBOOKS

TITLE	RETAIL PRICE	QTY	TOTAL
8 Steps for Highly Effective Negotiations #424	$14.95		
Assertiveness #4422	$14.95		
Balancing Career and Family #415	$14.95		
Delegate for Results #4592	$14.95		
Dynamic Communication Skills for Women #413	$14.95		
Exceptional Customer Service #4882	$14.95		
Fear & Anger: Slay the Dragons… #4302	$14.95		
Getting Things Done #4112	$14.95		
How to Coach an Effective Team #4308	$14.95		
How to De-Junk Your Life #4306	$14.95		
How to Handle Conflict and Confrontation #4952	$14.95		
How to Manage Your Boss #493	$14.95		
How to Supervise People #4102	$14.95		
How to Work with People #4032	$14.95		
Inspire & Motivate Through Performance Reviews #4232	$14.95		
Listen Up: Hear What's Really Being Said #4172	$14.95		
Motivation and Goal-Setting #4962	$14.95		
A New Attitude #4432	$14.95		
Parenting: Ward & June… #486	$14.95		
The Polished Professional #426	$14.95		
The Power of Innovative Thinking #428	$14.95		
The Power of Self-Managed Teams #4222	$14.95		
Powerful Communication Skills #4132	$14.95		
Powerful Leadership Skills for Women #463	$14.95		
Present with Confidence #4612	$14.95		
The Secret to Developing Peak Performers #4692	$14.95		
Self-Esteem: The Power to Be Your Best #4642	$14.95		
Shortcuts to Organized Files & Records #4307	$14.95		
The Stress Management Handbook #4842	$14.95		
Supreme Teams: How to Make Teams Work #4303	$14.95		
Techniques to Improve Your Writing Skills #460	$14.95		
Thriving on Change #4212	$14.95		
The Write Stuff #414	$14.95		

Sales Tax

All purchases subject to state and local sales tax. Questions? Call **1-800-258-7248**

Subtotal	$
Add 7% Sales Tax *(Or add appropriate state and local tax)*	$
Shipping and Handling *($3 one item; 50¢ each additional item)*	$
TOTAL	$